From Shallow Roots

From Shallow ROOTS

A How-to Guide for Creating, Growing, and Expanding the Life You Desire

Katie Elliott

First Edition

From Shallow Roots

A How-To Guide For Creating, Growing, and Expanding the Life you Desire

© 2023 Katie Elliott

Printed in the United States of America

First Edition

ISBN 979-8-218-24184-1 paperback
ISBN 979-8-218-24185-8 ebook
Library of Congress Control Number: 2023901225

Cover and Interior Design by:
Chris Treccani

Cover Artwork by:
Crea McKeen

Created with the Book to Millions® Method

DEDICATION

To My Beloved Children,

This book, "Shallow Roots," is dedicated to you – the very souls who breathed life back into me when I was suffocating under the weight of my past. You have been the sunlight that guided me out from my darkest hours, and the constant tide that carried me to new horizons. You gave me the purpose and courage to evolve, to change, to expand and create the life we now cherish.

You encouraged me to weave my stories into words, to explain how I journeyed through stormy seas to reach this haven of forgiveness, kindness, love, and connection. While this book only touches upon a fraction of my experiences, it encapsulates the essence of resilience that I hope you inherit.

There are many untold stories that are kept secret in the vaults of my heart; those are the ones too raw to share. But in each story echoed in these pages, and in every line, know this – your existence, your love, has been my greatest inspiration.

As you flip through these pages, remember that the strength you see in me resides in you too. You are resilient, capable, and endlessly worthy of all the beauty life has to offer. Even when I am no longer with you, this book will be a reminder that you carry within you the power to navigate life's turmoil.

Remember this: Your mama loves you more than words can capture.

To all my readers, I hope my stories offer you solace, insight, or a newfound perspective. Take from this what serves you best and may it benefit your journey in some small way.

With all my love.

TABLE OF CONTENTS

INTRODUCTION

Everyone that knows me has always told me that I should write a book. I'm not a writer, but I wanted to share my stories, and I wanted to write a book for my kids. Initially, I wanted to title the book *Forward Thinking*. I'm a forward thinker, and I believe the only way to grow and expand your life is to continuously look forward and get into action.

But that changed one day as I was out for a hike. I live in the beautiful state of Oregon, and I love to take walks in the forest. I came across some giant sequoia trees—massive trees that reminded me of my life: The little girl I once was, the circumstances I grew up in, and the woman I've become.

I experienced serious childhood traumas and sexual abuse. I'm not a Harvard graduate or a great scholar—I was a special ed kid in school, and I required a lot of help. In fact, I barely received my associate's degree when I was pregnant with my second child at the age of 25. I didn't learn to read with any kind of understanding until my late 20s. As a young mom, I was diagnosed with a heart condition. Yet despite all the difficulties life brought my way, I've created an amazing life for myself and my family, and here I am writing a book to share my story.

As I hiked that day in the forest among those giant trees, I came across one that had been uprooted. I stopped and stood under its shallow root system. A giant sequoia can stand 275 feet high, have a circumference of over 100 feet, and weigh in at an incredible 2.7 million pounds. But despite a sequoia's massiveness, its root system is broad and shallow, expanding to reach more than 100 feet in all directions. Sequoias are survivalists.

In the middle of the forest on that special day, surrounded by those giant trees, I connected the shallow root system with my life. I was born into and raised in very difficult situations, but I'm a survivor. I created a life for myself by spreading out in all directions—meeting new people, having new experiences, and forging new environments that continuously improve my life.

In that moment I realized I was born and raised in a narrow and deeply rooted system, the reason I was standing there on that day the person I was, was because I embraced the shallow root system. In that moment I decided to change the title of the book. It doesn't matter where you start out in life; what matters is creating, growing, and expanding your life through a root system that spreads out, allowing you to move forward. I believe we're here to help each other. We're here to grow, to expand, to stretch ourselves and stretch others.

Out of the crucible of life—the circumstances and people I've encountered—I've developed the skills of listening, seeing situations, and reframing them.

As a life coach, I help others reframe their stories. When we're stuck and going through hard times, we often fail to see the truth because of the stories we're telling ourselves. We're unable to reframe our situations in a positive way so we can continue to expand and grow. When we're stuck and unable to move forward, we feel hopeless.

In my coaching practice, I help clients reframe their circumstances. I help them find something good in what they're facing so they can get unstuck. I usually ask clients a series of questions to help them see that what they're worried about or fearful of might be a catalyst for them to move forward and continue creating, growing, and expanding the life they desire. When we reframe things, we can shift our attitudes, thoughts, and emotions, get unstuck, and take action. If we want to move forward, it's up to us. If we really want to change our lives, we have the power to do so—no matter what our circumstances may be.

I've divided this book into four key areas that shape our lives: Our attitudes, thoughts, emotions, and actions. Within these key areas, I share my stories and provide tools to help you reflect, reframe, and get into forward action.

My clients tell me that I have a no-nonsense approach to communication and a knack for creative problem-solving. This book reflects my approach to coaching. It provides a tool kit for you to use. It has been designed for you to write in and record your big dreams. I hope my personal stories will show you how someone who came from nothing is living a special life—and doing it using a tool that we all share—our brain.

Our thoughts and beliefs are part of us. No matter what your circumstances are right now, you're not alone. I hope you can relate to my story and that it will provide you with tools to pick yourself up and design the life you want. I hope you'll say, "STOP!" to any old story that's been playing in your mind—no matter how long it's been running. I hope you'll join the humans who say, "Enough!" to the past, and I hope you'll welcome the person you're meant to be.

You are incredibly powerful; you have the power to continue to grow, always. Stretch yourself. Be like the sequoia trees, expanding their shallow roots. Grow, expand, and create the life you desire!

With Love, Katie

Part 1:

Attitude

"It is our attitude toward events, not events themselves, which we can control."
—EPICTETUS

Attitude is the key that defines us. It is the lens through which we view the world around us. It's the result of our thoughts, beliefs, and experiences, and it colors our perception of every situation we encounter. Our attitude is not only a *mental* state but also a *physical* and *emotional* state that influences how we engage with the world.

CHAPTER 1:

Maintain an Attitude
of Gratitude

E ven in the most difficult circumstances, I have always been grateful. But it took some very particular circumstances to help me understand the true meaning of gratitude and to see that our attitude has the power to change the direction of our lives.

When you have an attitude of gratitude, you approach life with a sense of appreciation and thankfulness for the good things that come your way *and* the challenges you encounter. You focus on what you *have* rather than what you *lack*, and you recognize the positive aspects of your life even when times are tough.

No time in my life was tougher than when I thought I was going to die.

It was 2002. My husband, Jesse, and I were living away from family in Arizona, where Jesse was in the middle of a program to earn his doctor of physical therapy (DPT) degree. Grad school meant that Jesse pretty much didn't exist—he was always in class or studying. I was a young mom to our firstborn, Elijah—who at that time was a very energetic toddler. It *felt* like I was a single mom with no outside support.

Then—it seemed like it was overnight—I began to have a hard time walking up the stairs to our apartment. It confused me. I was young and healthy—or so I thought. But the stairs would kick my ass every time. I needed more and more sleep, and I couldn't keep up with Elijah.

One blisteringly hot day, I was with Elijah at the apartment complex pool. An acquaintance was there—another mom whose husband was a doctor. They were living in our apartment building while their house was under construction.

"How are you doing?" she asked.

Of course, we usually say, "I'm fine, thanks" in conversations like that. But I was feeling vulnerable.

"Oh, not well," I blurted. "I'm super tired all the time." "That doesn't sound right," she replied.

Looking back, I'm so grateful that she acted on her gut. She reached out to her husband—the doctor—who graciously came to see me at our apartment that night. He asked me a few questions, then told me that my symptoms didn't add up. He asked me to come by his office so he could run some tests.

The next day, I went to his office, and they ran some diagnostic tests and drew blood. What came next was even more frightening.

"I need to admit you to the hospital," he said. I was terrified. I called Jesse. He had to leave in the middle of class to get Elijah.

It was all so unexpected. My life was unfolding very differently from what we had planned. All of a sudden, I was in the hospital, and I didn't know what was going on. What was wrong with me? Was I going to die?

For the next few days, the doctors continued to run tests. My stepmom, bless her heart, had me on every prayer chain imaginable from the moment I was admitted to the hospital. In addition to having many people pray for me, a sweet friend overnighted me a book by Louise Hay titled *You Can Heal Your Life*. That little book was my salvation.

In *You Can Heal Your Life*, Louise Hay shares her story. I felt like I had so much in common with her. She, too, had a difficult childhood. She was abused and overcame many hardships. Not only did she heal her life—she also healed herself of cancer. She said you can heal almost anything if you go through the mental exercise of changing your thinking. The book was full of exercises, meditations, and affirmations that emphasized self-healing—the power of the mind to heal the body.

In between medical tests, I read that little book and started practicing the meditations and affirmations. I talked a lot with my Creator. I visualized getting stronger and stronger every day and being healed.

As I was in the hospital reading, hoping, and praying, Jesse wasn't able to visit very often because Elijah wasn't allowed in. We didn't have any family support nearby—no one who could watch our little guy while Jesse visited me. But on the day when the doctor was finally ready to give me my test results, some friends we'd met shortly after moving to Arizona offered to take care of Elijah so Jesse could be with me. I'm still so thankful for them—hearing my diagnosis alone, without Jesse, would have been so much harder.

When the doctor came in, he looked like he had been up all night. In a kindly way, he did his best to explain to us that my heart was not operating well and was slowly getting worse. I imagine that the news he had for a 22-year-old who was just starting her family—that she was probably going to die—might have made him lose some sleep.

"The best way I can explain it to you is that your heart got a cold," he told me. "Unfortunately, it's not like a normal cold where you make a full recovery."

Further complicating the situation, my blood pressure was extremely low. Medications normally prescribed for my condition were off the table because they would have lowered my blood pressure even further.

We just sat there, speechless. What was going to happen? What was I going to do? "What are my options?" I asked finally.

Looking at the doctor's face, I knew they weren't good.

"You should get your name on the list for a heart transplant."

What are my chances of getting a heart transplant? I thought. *Here I am, 22 years old, putting my name on the heart transplant list!*

The doctor said they would continue to monitor me as the team formulated a plan. When he left the room, I buried my head in Jesse's chest and cried my eyes out.

There is no way this is happening. I've been so healthy all my life. There is no way this is happening.

These thoughts went through my mind, over and over again.

I'm the happiest I've ever been. I've got my little boy. I'm married to the best human in the world. And now I'm going to die.

Jesse and I just didn't believe it.

"I want to get better. I want to heal," I told him. "Jesse, I'm not going to die. I'm going to get better."

Jesse, being the practical human he is, smiled at me and kissed my head.

When he left that evening, I felt empty. I had a wonderful life. We had plans. We had made a new beginning in Arizona. And now it was going to all end.

I couldn't sleep. Instead, I read and prayed. I took out *You Can Heal Your Life* and began to do heart meditations, over and over.

"I'm not going to die," I told God. "I can heal my life. I can be better."

I had a son to raise and it was not my time to go. There—in the middle of the night—I decided this *wasn't* happening to me. I closed my eyes and imagined my son older. I imagined all the things we would do together. I clung to those visions as I went through the meditations and affirmations. I held that book so close to me. I was going to heal my life.

The next day, the doctors set up a treatment plan for me and sent me home. I had to go in every few days for testing, but they didn't see any need to keep me from Elijah. I could be at home if I could get help with him. I was so happy to get home and snuggle with my little guy. I was so grateful to have such a beautiful family.

My sister-in-law, Tiffany, came to stay with us for two weeks, caring for me and cooking and cleaning. She made some real sacrifices to be with us. She was very pregnant at the time, and she left her own daughter at home with my brother. Money was tight, so we kept the air conditioner off for most of the day. Our little apartment was *flaming* hot.

Tiffany's visit allowed Jesse and I to get some time alone and have some long conversations. We had so much to think about. Our whole world—our plans, everything we were working toward—had changed overnight. Was I going to get better? Was I going to die? Would he finish his doctoral program? We needed to pivot, hoping I would recover my health. We talked about our future and what it might look like with all these unknowns.

Jesse was in the second year of his doctoral program. We decided that he should finish grad school while Elijah and I moved back home to Oregon. We'd be separated for a while, but at least he would have a good job to take care of us once he graduated. There was no way I could stay in Arizona with Elijah without family or anyone else around to help.

Tiffany helped us pack up our apartment. My dad drove down in a U-Haul. He and Jesse loaded up the truck. As we drove off— my dad, me, and Elijah—we waved goodbye to Jesse. I remember thinking, *I am getting stronger, and I am going to heal.*

Back in Oregon, Elijah and I moved in with my brother and Tiffany and their young daughter. Although I knew I had a long road ahead to recovery, I was grateful for such loving care. My brother and sister-in-law gave me so much love and help with Elijah.

Every day, I continued following the meditations in *You Can Heal Your Life.* I clung to that book and prayed: "I am healing my heart. I am healing my life." I focused on owning my life.

This isn't the end. I knew it. I felt it.

I didn't focus on where I was—I focused on where I was going. I didn't dwell on the fact that I was sick. Every day I got up and pushed a little harder. I went for longer walks. I played with Elijah. To a certain extent, my son saved my life, because I had to take care of him. I just continued on the path of caring for him.

Slowly, I got better. I was still following the doctors' treatment plan, which included monthly echocardiograms. The tests improved, little by little, month by month. I kept on visualizing and meditating. And in the end, I never got added to the heart transplant list.

The cardiologist couldn't understand my improvement. "You know what, Katie," he said, "We can't explain any of this, but you seem to be getting better."

Jesse finished his coursework and came home. It was a beautiful reunion, and we've never looked back. We just kept moving forward from there.

My recovery was slow. When I first moved back to Oregon, I couldn't walk up a flight of stairs. But over the course of that year, I slowly healed. I healed to the point where I was approved to have another baby, years later.

As human beings, we are connected, and we're connected to the universe. Once we tap into those connections, anything's possible. Through the ordeal of my illness, I felt like I transcended to another level of spirituality—that's the best I can describe it. I knew that I was in control. The life that I'd been given—this gift—I could do *anything* with it. I wasn't controlled by outside influences; I was in control, from the inside out. My input would determine my output—what I would get out of life. That was a real awakening.

Seeing my improvement, I started to believe wholeheartedly that I had the power to heal my body. That was a big moment in my life—learning how we are connected to the world around us—and it felt like a miracle. To this day, based on my personal experience, I believe that due to the stories that we tell ourselves over the years and the circumstances that challenge our lives play a large part in how disease shows up in our body.

Some people equate miracle and luck, but they're different. With luck, you're at the right place at the right time. With a miracle, you're a participant. And with my heart, I participated. I didn't just lay there doing nothing while my heart got better. I filled my brain with positive thoughts, and I enlisted my friends and my family to send healing thoughts, too. It was a miracle, but we all *participated*; we made the miracle happen.

We have beliefs that keep us stuck in our stories. If I had listened to the doctors and not taken the initiative to heal myself, I think I would have died.

In other words, if I simply trusted other people to take care of me, they would have done a subpar job. Not that I have anything against them—it's just that they would have done what they knew. And if I was simply trusting others, my friend's gift of *You Can Heal Your Life* wouldn't have served me.

To me, the biggest lesson is that I never accepted what I was told. I never accepted that I was going to die unless I got a heart transplant. I never felt that any of that was true. And I rejected those ideas—I rejected the whole concept.

The power of the mind, my connection to another source, to God—I don't know how to explain it—but spiritually, I tapped into a power greater than myself, something beyond my understanding. It was very powerful, and I still lean into that spirituality today. It totally changed my life.

When my life isn't going the way I want it to, I return to the same practices I began back in the hospital in Arizona. I take time to connect with myself. I connect to this force that's greater than myself. Just like when I was in the hospital and refused to accept that I was going to die as a truth, I reject the negative and then project what I want to be true.

When I was ill, I continued the treatment plan the doctor gave me, but I also visualized my future and prayed for my health.

As I watched Elijah and my niece, Lindsey, play together, I remember thinking, *I'm going to be here for all of this. I'm going to be here for weddings. I'm not going to die. I'm not going anywhere.* I feel like that focus on the future almost *pulled* me out of my illness.

Throughout that time, I felt so much gratitude for everyone who was there for me during my healing journey. I continuously held an attitude of gratitude.

To my neighbor in the apartment complex, for her response when I told her how lousy I was feeling.

To her husband for inviting me into his office to run tests.

I was thankful for all the doctors at the hospital, even if they weren't sure how to move forward. It didn't matter. I was grateful for their knowledge, their ability to connect with me, their consistent care and diligence. They gave me a treatment plan and researched my case—they did everything in their power to help me get well.

To my stepmom, for getting me on every prayer list imaginable.

To my girlfriend for sending me *You Can Heal Your Life*—a book that gave me hope for healing.

To my sister-in-law, Tiffany, for making huge sacrifices while pregnant so she could come and take care of me; and to my brother, for loving me so much and encouraging Tiffany to come.

So much love and so much support went into my healing.

My recovery was truly a miracle. I became healthy and vibrant again, and even had another baby! But it wasn't a miracle without work. I went into deliberate action. I worked with the doctors, and I worked with my faith to take care of my health and get better.

When the doctors said my heart wouldn't heal, I started to ask why? My understanding of what I heard was that the heart doesn't act like other muscles in the body. If you pull your bicep, you can rehab it and get your strength back. Once your heart is damaged, it doesn't come back.

I didn't believe them. It didn't make any sense to me. I thought, *It's a muscle. It's got to come back.* And I decided I was going to get better.

There were two pieces to the puzzle. First, I knew I wouldn't be able to get a heart transplant. I was on state insurance, and we didn't have much money. I figured I would be about the last person to get a heart transplant. Second, I received Louise Hay's book, and I identified with her story. Reading about how she was able to heal gave me strength. *Maybe,* I thought, *I can heal my heart.*

Between those two pieces—knowing that my chances of help from the medical world were low and finding hope in *You Can Heal Your Life*—I chose to pour everything into using the book's tools. I focused all my faith on healing, and my heart started to get better. The power of the mind is beyond our imagination.

Nobody cares more about your health, marriage, kids, or money than you do. If you truly want to move the needle and make a change, you have to say, "This is my life, and I'm going to own it. I am grateful for all that I have today. I'm going to make it."

Reflection Questions

What's going on in my life right now that's challenging?

1.

2.

3.

What can I do to adopt an attitude of gratitude?

How can I bring more gratitude into my life?

Personal Reflections:

CHAPTER 2:

Take Responsibility

Having an attitude of taking responsibility means being proactive, taking ownership of your actions, and working toward finding solutions to problems rather than blaming others for your circumstances.

When I was 13, my life took an unexpected turn. It was a Monday morning, and I rode the bus to go to school. When I got to school, I felt like something was off.

Over the weekend, I had spent some time with a girlfriend. I told her how pissed off I was at the world. I told her about what was happening at home with my stepdad—how he was being inappropriate with me. I really wanted it to stop. As I shared this secret with her, I was so angry. All I wanted was for him to leave me alone. At least talking with her helped me feel a little better.

I didn't think she would betray my confidence. But on Monday morning as I arrived at school, I saw a police car in the parking lot, and I knew immediately that they were there for me. My friend must have told somebody what I had confided in her.

I was pissed off. I went into the hallway and grabbed her. "Is that police car here for me?" I demanded.

She looked at me with the saddest eyes. "Katie, you can't stay there."

"What did you do? Why did you tell someone? You're ruining my life," I screamed at her.

I ran out into the school courtyard and called my mom from the pay phone. When she answered, all I could do was scream, "Mom, come pick me up! Come pick me up right now!"

"Katie, what's going on?" she asked.

I told her the police were there for me, that they were going to take me away, and that she had to come and get me.

"You have to come! You have to come get me right now!" I pleaded. She couldn't come get me.

I hung up. One of my best friends was nearby, and he came over when he saw me crying hysterically.

"I can't do this," I said. "I need to run away. They're going to take me away from my family." He looked at me. "You can do this," he said.

I knew he was right. I couldn't keep lying. This wasn't the first time the police had come to my school. In elementary school, I must have shared something with a counselor or teacher that alerted them that I was being abused. I got called in for special meetings with the police that I called "wellness checks." I always told them I was fine.

That Monday in middle school, I was *not* fine. I was scared. The girl I had talked to over the weekend had betrayed my confidence and shared my secret. The police were there for another "wellness check." I asked my friend to come with me, and he did. That gave me the strength I needed.

When we walked back into the school, we were taken into a little room that smelled like paper. The room was clean and sterile, a simple school room. There was one table with a few tiny metal chairs—the chairs were so cold.

We sat down. Two people sat across from us, a man, and a woman, looking very official. I didn't recognize them from the school.

"Katie, it's okay. You can tell us what's happening," the woman said.

I looked at my friend. He had the sweetest eyes. "Katie, you can do this," he said.

I broke down crying. I couldn't stop. They asked me about my stepdad, but all I could do was cry. They asked more questions, but I just shook my head and cried some more.

Instead of going to school that day, I rode in a police car to Child Protective Services.

I felt so betrayed. I hadn't done anything wrong. I was angry at my girlfriend for having shared my secret.

Child Protective Services called my parents and told them I wasn't coming home. Instead, I got sent to a foster home. It was horrible. I wanted to go home. I didn't belong in foster care.

As soon as I got to the foster home, I ran away. The police caught me and took me back to the foster home. They gave me a choice. I could stay in the foster home, or I could go live with my dad.

I didn't want to live with my dad. My parents divorced when I was a newborn. My dad had remarried and had a new family—all boys—and I didn't feel like I belonged. I didn't get along with my stepmom or my stepbrothers, and I always felt like an outsider when I visited. I didn't have my own room, and I slept on the couch. As I got older, I visited less and less. So, to go live with my dad would have been like going to live with strangers. I didn't feel like that was my family.

I wanted my life to go back to the way it had been. I wanted to be with my mother and my brothers. I had an older brother and two younger brothers who were my whole life and I missed them so much.

After a while, there was a custody hearing. My mom and dad and a bunch of other people were there. We all sat around an oval table with a judge. The judge asked my parents questions. My mom looked completely helpless. She didn't have a clue what to do; she was alone. My dad exuded confidence and had an answer for everything.

It was clear that they wouldn't let me go back to living with my mom and my brothers. She couldn't even answer any of the judge's questions. When we left the courtroom, I walked down the stairs with my mother, holding her hand for dear life.

She went to her car and pulled out a few things she had brought from my room—a teddy bear and some other things I loved. From the day the police took me away from school, I had never been able to go back home. On the sidewalk with my mom, holding the things she had brought for me—that meant the world to me.

We sat there. My mom was crying. "Katie," she said, "What are we going to do? What are we going to do?"

I'll never forget that moment. There were cars and people going by, but to me, everything fell silent. It was like the world stood still. My mom cried for what seemed to be an eternity. Then she asked me question after question, and I realized at that moment the depth of my mom. I saw her for who she really was, the most loving and caring person who had experienced so much pain, struggles and challenges in her life. She just wasn't equipped with the tools and didn't know what to do to move us forward. I then realized just how much my mom loved me, but no one was coming to save me I was all alone. I would have to figure things out for myself.

By then, I finally realized that I couldn't go home with my mom and my brothers. I didn't want to be in that little house with my stepdad. My options were to live with my dad or be a constant runaway— homeless and who knows what else. As hard as it was to accept it, my dad was my only hope. At that moment, I knew I had to take full responsibility for my life moving forward.

I was headed back to the foster home while Child Protective Services arranged for my transition to live with my dad.

My mom, my brothers and stepdad moved away immediately—they disappeared. The authorities had started to investigate the same day I had been taken away from school and from my mom. While I was in foster care, my stepdad had gone into hiding. After the custody hearing, they moved away. I didn't know where they were or how to get in touch with them.

I moved in with my dad and his family. That took me in a whole new direction. I quickly learned to navigate a new life. In my mom's house, I did what I wanted; I came and went as I pleased. Now I had rules to follow, and I had to deal with the consequences of not following the rules. I wasn't used to such a structured life. I was belligerent. My stepmom, bless her heart, did her absolute best. I was sassy and talked back. She tried to love me, but I didn't want to be loved by her. All I wanted was to be with my mom.

It was hard to take responsibility for anything that had happened to me to that point. I had been through so much. I had been taken away from my family, and I felt very much like a victim.

Rightfully so—I had definitely been victimized.

I could have continued on as a victim. I could have stayed in my own pity party, feeling sorry for myself. Actually, I did that for a long time.

But somewhere along the way, little by little, I learned to take responsibility for my life. I learned that I could control my life.

However, my first step in the direction of control was to consider suicide. I thought, *I don't like my life, and I don't see any way out. Let's just end this whole thing.*

As dark as that is, it's a important to bring up. We all want to feel like we're in control of our lives. We're a species that wants to be in control. I couldn't control my circumstances, but I could control myself.

I have control—I can end this, I thought. *I can kill myself.*

I attempted suicide multiple times. Thank God I'm still here today. My suicide attempts at least drew attention so I could get help.

My stepmom made sure I went to all my therapy sessions. She and my dad worked hard to get me what they thought I needed; they did their best to help me. I was a troubled kid.

My mom had done the best she could, too. My life to age 13 was like living in Disney World compared to how she had grown up. She was born to an intellectually disabled mother. From the time she was a newborn, Child Protective Services was visiting several times a week. At three years old, she and her siblings went into foster care. Later, she was adopted—but her adoptive mother was brutal. At the age of 15 my mom fell in love and got pregnant. No baby is ever a mistake and due to the circumstances in her life at the time she had to raise the baby on her own. It was so hard for her; she was so young. My mom did the best she could in raising all of us.

To live the life I wanted to live, I needed to take responsibility for my life. I needed to design and create the life I wanted. I lost everything I had loved and known—leaving my mother and my brothers, going into foster care, and then going to live with my dad.

I learned a lot of valuable lessons during that time. Sometimes, we're on our own. We've got to dig deep, reflect, and realize that it's up to us to change.

I started seventh grade in a new school, living in a new world. I was different from the kids at school. They seemed so sweet and innocent. I started the year with half my head shaved, and I was pissed off at the world.

Reflecting on that time, I realized that I wanted to be known, to be heard, to have opinions and have them be considered valid. I wanted to live on my own terms. But I didn't know how to articulate any of that. However, I had learned that I could control a couple of things—I could take responsibility for myself and my actions, for my life and the direction I wanted it to go.

Several weeks into the school year, an eighth-grade girl who had started the year with us left and went to high school. She was the direct opposite of me. She seemed to have everything that I didn't have. She was the most popular girl in school, and she was drop-dead gorgeous.

When she left, I thought, *how did she do that?*

I saw a doorway out. I was one of the oldest kids in the school—I didn't belong in junior high—I belonged in high school. I thought it was a long shot, but I wanted to be out of the situation I was in. So, I got up the courage to go to my counselor.

"Hey, I don't want to be here anymore. How do I get out of here?" He and my parents talked, and they devised a plan.

"Well, Katie," the counselor told me, "If you hate it here that much and want to get out and move up to high school, you have to get straight A's for the first half of seventh grade, and then you have to get straight A's the second half of the year doing eighth-grade work. If you can do that, we'll move you up to high school."

I was in special classes to help with my reading. The idea of getting straight A's and doing it at the eighth-grade level seemed nearly impossible. I didn't think I would be able to do it. But I wanted out so badly that I was determined to at least *try*. I wanted to go to high school!

I gave it my all. I took on all the responsibility. I stayed after school, met with counselors, and got help. I did everything I could. I completely dug into it. I pushed and pushed, learned how to read, got straight A's, and then got straight A's doing eighth-grade work.

The most curious aspect of that whole time is that I didn't know what I was doing. I was acting out of desperation. But looking back, I can break down the steps I took. I saw someone who was different, and I wanted what she had. That lit a fire in me and got me moving in the direction I wanted to go—high school.

Out of curiosity, I asked questions. That brought me information. With that information, I was able to formulate a plan and take responsibility for executing it in order to achieve what that eighth-grade girl had achieved.

How does a kid who's in special classes for slow learners turn things around and get straight A's? It wasn't because I believed I was smart or believed I could get straight A's. Knowing there was a way out of a situation I didn't want to be in, I believed I could take on the responsibility to make my escape. I was focused on where I was *going*, not on where I was or what I was doing.

Up until that point, my life in school followed the status quo. I did what I had to do to get by. I didn't need to prove anything. I think I was always smart, but I had been told I was dumb. I hadn't had any reason to challenge that orthodoxy. Given the opportunity, I rose to the occasion. When I needed help, I asked questions and reached out.

In the beginning phases of change, it's crucial to find a way to get unstuck. Find professionals, mentors, and coaches to help you. I had my parents and teachers, the school counselor, and therapy, helping and guiding me.

What do you need to change course? Who can you reach out to for help?

> **You are the only one that can take responsibility to change your life. When I learned how to take responsibility for my life, everything changed.**

We all fall into unexpected circumstances. We can become victims, go with the status quo, and accept the circumstances. We can blame everyone and everything for our situations and stay locked in a self-destructive cycle. The bad things that happen to us that are out of our control, but we need to move forward and heal. I could have continued to be angry at the world, gone on as a belligerent runaway and a dropout. But when I realized I needed to take responsibility for myself, my life began to change. Taking responsibility means working hard to get to what you want. It may not come easy, but you have to take the first step. I had to work hard to get my grades up and move up to high school. The drive I felt to get to high school got me through some of the tough times.

The first step I took was to take responsibility for myself. Although I was a kid, I realized that running away and not facing my life wouldn't help me. The second step was to ask how I could leave junior high like the other girl and go to high school. The third step was to meet with my parents and the school counselor and make a plan. The fourth step was to meet the conditions that had been given to me for moving up to high school.

The only way forward from where you are now is to start taking responsibility for your life.

The things that had happened to me weren't my fault. It wasn't my fault that I was at my dad's or that my mom had abandoned me, taken my brothers, and left. But what happened next was up to me. I could say, "This is my life. It's my responsibility to make it whatever I want it to be."

This is the biggest gift I've ever given myself—taking responsibility for myself, moving forward, and not looking back. It doesn't do me any good to look back, and it won't do you any good, either.

> **Take responsibility for your life, for your day, for your actions. You need to own them.**

When you do something wrong, apologize and move on. Quit dwelling in the past. Quit blaming your parents, society, or your boss. Just stop. It's your life—you only get one.

Do you choose to live your life as a victim?

Do you choose to have the direction of your life dictated by things that happened to you in the past?

Or do you choose to take control of your life? You can take responsibility for your life and say, "I am here, right now and I'm going to move forward from here. I know how I want to live my life." There's no point in looking backward. We all have to start from right here, where we are. We have to look forward. Take responsibility from here on out. Your life will unfold in ways you've never imagined simply because of this one change.

Reflection Questions

What situations or events in your life are hard to take responsibility for?

1.

2.

3.

What are you telling yourself that prevents you from taking responsibility for your life?

Personal Reflections:

CHAPTER 3:

Be Curious: Ask Questions

My husband says he'd probably be working for the hospital if it wasn't for my crazy curiosity and all the questions I asked about how we could open our own clinic. Jesse and I were at a crossroads in our lives. He was on the verge of finishing his physical therapy clinical rotations in Oregon, my health was improving after a long struggle, and little Elijah was growing more amazing every day.

Because of my heart condition, the thought of having another child seemed like a distant dream. But I couldn't shake the feeling that maybe—just maybe—it was a possibility. I decided to ask my cardiologist about it during a routine appointment. He looked at my chart and, with a warm smile, reassured me that my heart was strong enough to withstand another pregnancy.

In my car afterward, tears streamed down my face as I finally allowed myself to grieve what I had almost lost. I had faced the possibility of dying and not being able to have the life I wanted.

Now I learned that I could have another child. I couldn't wait to share the news with Jesse. His eyes lit up with joy and surprise, and we embraced, picturing the family we had always dreamed of.

Jesse started receiving job offers as he completed his clinical rotations. I'll never forget our laughter—tinged with disbelief—as we looked at the low salaries they offered.

I playfully tossed the papers aside. "Jesse, you should start your own practice instead of working for someone." He gave me his signature look—a sideways glance, eyes narrowed, and an expression that says, "Girl, you are crazy" tinged with "But you might also be right."

With his blessing, I was off to the races looking into how to make a clinic—our clinic—a reality. I knew we needed something like that if we wanted to have a more abundant life. We had student loans, a child to raise, and I desperately wanted another child. We wanted to be able to enjoy time together as a family and give back to others.

Although my illness had forced us to change course to some extent, we knew that we had made the right decision when I moved back to Oregon and Jesse stayed in Arizona to finish his doctorate.

Now, Jesse was back in Oregon, a doctor of physical therapy. We had planned our lives around this moment. But it was soon clear that our goals and dreams were going to require a salary larger than the offer Jesse ended up accepting. I couldn't shake the idea that we needed to open a clinic. Jesse worked long hours, and we were barely getting by. When we talked about it with friends and acquaintances, we'd hear things like, "Well, what did you think he was going to make?" or "You'll have to get better at budgeting," or—my favorite—"We all have to put our time in; that's just how the world works."

Bullshit, I thought. I knew there had to be a better way to create and grow the life we wanted. Some people get on with life quicker than others, and I was going to figure out how to be one of them.

I refused to accept that Jesse would work for 40 years making just enough to pay off school loans and afford a basic living. He sacrificed so much for us. When he wasn't in school or studying, he was working and doing everything he could to give us the best life. I didn't know exactly what to do, but others had figured out how to create an abundant life and so would I.

As I started looking into how people got a head start on the journey to financial freedom, I found a common thread: They were entrepreneurs. I barely knew what the word *entrepreneur* meant (I still have a hard time saying it), but I realized that people who got ahead of their main salary were entrepreneurs.

By asking around, I also discovered that people made money in real estate. They bought homes and sold them or kept them as rentals. I knew all about rentals . . . because I was a renter.

I went to my dad and discussed every new idea I learned. He was a huge help to my education on how people got ahead financially. He had worked in several family businesses, then got a big break with an insurance company where he worked as an agent. Later, he left to start his own company with a partner. He was smart and had business sense, and I felt comfortable asking his advice.

When I told him I thought Jesse should open his own clinic, he was in full support and mentored me. He taught me how to engage with my community, what it means to be an entrepreneur, and how to get started.

Everything begins with asking questions and being curious about your options. I've furthered my life in every direction by simply stopping to consider:

- What do I think I know?
- What do I *not* know?
- What do I think I know but really *don't* know?

Often, we don't get the information we need to move forward because we don't ask questions. I had a million questions about the clinic. We were young and had never opened a clinic—not to mention that we'd never been entrepreneurs of any sort. It would be a challenge, but it was a challenge I was ready to take on. I never stopped asking questions, exploring possibilities and checking to ensure that our choices were taking us in the right direction.

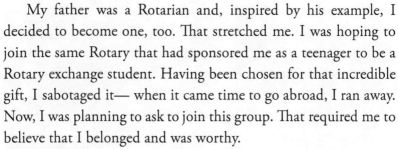

You are only limited by the quality of your questions and the extent of your curiosity.

My father was a Rotarian and, inspired by his example, I decided to become one, too. That stretched me. I was hoping to join the same Rotary that had sponsored me as a teenager to be a Rotary exchange student. Having been chosen for that incredible gift, I sabotaged it— when it came time to go abroad, I ran away. Now, I was planning to ask to join this group. That required me to believe that I belonged and was worthy.

Believing in yourself in that way isn't something you *feel*; it's something you *choose*. I *felt* terrible—like I was crazy for even having the gall to walk into the club. I *felt* like I was in way over my head. But at the same time, I knew that it didn't matter how I felt. I took a deep breath and walked into the meeting.

When you want to join Rotary, you first attend a meeting as a guest. You can be a guest many times. I didn't just want to be a guest; I wanted to be a member. To become a member of Rotary, you don't fill out an application, pay a fee, and get a membership card. Your membership has to be proposed by another member without your knowledge. After your name is proposed in three meetings without anyone objecting, you're invited to submit an application. The whole process can take months. So, I had to believe in my worth many times before my father proposed my membership to the group.

My experience with Rotary mirrored many things in my life: When I put myself out there and believe that I belong, everything comes together. I was welcomed into Rotary with open arms and minimal joking about my teenage years.

As a Rotarian, I learned the importance of caring for our world, expanded my connections, and was surrounded by like-minded individuals who were committed to making a positive impact in the community. I was amazed by their stories of resilience and success, and I soaked up their wisdom like a sponge.

All these experiences taught me the value of asking questions, seeking answers beyond the obvious, and the power of building strong relationships.

As I grew more confident in my ability to contribute to the community, I realized that the connections I was making were essential to opening Jesse's clinic. I started attending events and meeting business people. I'd sit with them at breakfast or luncheon events and pick their brains. I didn't talk about myself—I asked what they did, asked them to talk about their experiences. I asked question after question—"What do you do?" and "How did you get started?" Then I'd dig deeper. I was constantly making dis-coveries. For example, I learned that we needed liability insurance for the clinic. All those conversations led to education, to learning aspects of business that I didn't know anything about.

At one event, I sat at a table full of attorneys. I don't know anything about practicing law, and lawyers can be really intimidat-ing. But there was an empty seat, and I took it. I didn't have much to say about the legal world, but I had learned that we all have something to share. So, I asked my questions and picked up some nuggets, and they asked me questions about being a mom and family life. I *did* have something to offer them.

We all have something to share.

Another thing that helped me as I researched opening a clinic was that I didn't make it about me. I was 24 years old, and my big-gest challenge was getting people to take me seriously. If I thought about myself and all the things I didn't know, I would have been too scared to ask questions.

A personal challenge was that I lived in a community of people who knew my history. They had watched me grow up, and they knew I had been a troubled teenager. They knew all about my family struggles. I had to push through all the assumptions about who I was and prove that I had grown up, was strong, and could stand on my own two feet.

It wasn't easy. Many times, I wanted to crawl into a hole and hide. What were they thinking and saying about me? It would have been easy to say, "Yes, I'm that same troubled teenager." But I *wasn't* that person. I had to get up every day and prove them wrong. I wanted to succeed. I wanted Jesse to open his clinic.

With the guidance of a phenomenal mentor, Jesse began to build his practice. He worked part- time for her and part-time for himself. On weekends, he worked at an assisted living facility. He seemed to be working all the time. We were saving up to open up our clinic, and it was so hard on all of us.

I've always had a can-do approach to life. I believe anything is possible. The more typical approach to life is to accept information without questioning it, to take things at face value without examining their validity or exploring alternative perspectives. Many people don't seek out new knowledge or challenge their own beliefs.

When I was in the hospital for my heart condition, I wanted to live. I didn't want to die. I questioned everything. I stepped out of my comfort zone because I wanted to live. I explored the possibility that the information in *You Can Heal Your Life* could help. I constantly asked questions of the doctors and other personnel caring for my health. Although I'd always been curious and asked questions, my illness fine-tuned those traits. It challenged me—I had to continue asking questions, work with my doctors on a treatment plan, and get better. I took the same approach to opening the clinic. I was determined to keep asking questions until I got the answers I needed for planning and opening the clinic.

With my children and in life, I'm always asking questions. I'm intentional about asking questions because I want to know more. This process of asking questions as I listen opens a whole dialogue and a safe place for my kids to be able to share. My kids are probably the most curious people I know. When they were little, their curiosity made things challenging, because everything out of their mouth started with "Why . . . ?" I remember wanting to say, "Because I said so!" so many times. However, teaching my children to be curious and ask questions has had great rewards. Both Elijah and Ella, my daughter, have experienced life in ways they wouldn't have if it weren't for asking, "Why?" or "Why not?" or "What's another way?"

I've gotten so far in my life just by asking questions. I meet people who haven't gotten very far in their lives, and a big reason for that is that they're not curious. They're not asking questions.

Instead, they're concerned about being right. They're thinking about what they're going to say to you rather than listening to you and formulating a question to keep the discussion going.

I think most people are content with closed dialogue because they're ready to tell you something. I approach things with a question. I ask others to tell me more:

- "Explain that to me."
- "How does that work?"
- "Tell me what you're passionate about."

I'm in a constant state of curiosity. When people ask me things, I get to share—then we learn from each other, because we're curious about each other. Asking questions is a fun way to live; it's full of open conversations. Everyone likes to talk about themselves, so draw it out of them— ask questions!

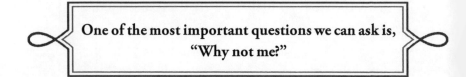

One of the most important questions we can ask is, "Why not me?"

We all have limiting beliefs. We get stuck in how we think of ourselves, in our own stories. As you go through life being curious and asking questions, the number one question I encourage you to ask is, "Why not me?"

Asking questions educates you and introduces you to new ideas and ways of doing things.

I was determined to open a physical therapy clinic. I was tired of seeing my husband work long hours and struggle to pay off student loans. I knew that being an entrepreneur would be challenging but would ultimately give us a better future.

Reflection Questions

What is something you'd like to learn how to do?

1.

2.

3.

Who do you need to meet and what questions do you need to ask?

Personal Reflections:

CHAPTER 4:

Be Abundant

As I made new connections through the Rotary Club, Jesse's referrals were increasing. He was able to stop working the weekend job, and the dream of moving outside his shared office space seemed within reach. I encouraged him to look for a place to lease.

Jesse and I are very different. He wanted to branch out, but he also was afraid of going all in and not being able to provide what we needed. I don't know if it's simply because we're wired differently or if it's because we have different levels of belief in ourselves, but I never worried for a second. I knew he would be successful because there was no other option. To be honest, even if he had said he didn't want to open a clinic, I probably wouldn't have heard him. I had decided he would grow. I didn't know *how* it would happen, but I was determined that it *would* happen.

The dream of opening a clinic kept coming back to one thing: We didn't have the money to get into a lease. No one was going to take on all the risk. We had to come up with more savings if we wanted to make the clinic a reality.

My unwillingness to leave things at that drove me to ask more questions. I asked questions of fellow Rotarians, women in my book club—anyone I thought might be able to guide us. My pitch went like this: "Jesse and I don't have much savings, but his referrals are picking up, and I believe he can have a successful clinic if he can just get a bigger space."

One day, my dad suggested that I talk with some of the bankers in Rotary. "Honey, you'll never know if you don't ask," he told me. "The worst that can happen is they'll say no."

I hate the word *no*, and I'll go to great lengths to avoid hearing it. But I decided to ask anyway. I casually mentioned our dilemma to one of the bankers at a lunch meeting.

"Why don't you come to the bank?" he said. "Let's discuss it."

I was overjoyed. What I heard was, "Yes, I will help you." Of course, that's not what he had said, but that's what I *felt*, and that was the story I decided was true. This banker was going to help get us the money.

I went to his office and poured my heart out. "We don't have much, but we work hard," I said. I told him what we had done to that point and promised him that we wouldn't let him down. When I finished, he asked me to write a proposal.

I left feeling totally defeated. I didn't even know what a proposal was, not to mention how to write one. I told Jesse about the meeting, and we came up with a one-page written proposal. It explained how we planned to grow Jesse's practice one referral at a time. We included our projected income and what we thought our expenses might be. In retrospect, there is no way that proposal should have earned us a loan—yet that's exactly what happened.

The banker judged us on our character and took a huge risk. And, of course, we didn't let him down.

Once we had secured a loan, we needed to find a home for the clinic. There was a cute little place for lease on a corner close to our home. It was perfect for our clinic.

On our way home one evening, I asked Jesse, "What do you think about that place on the corner?"

"Let's call and see about it," he said.

But as we passed by it, we noticed someone inside.

"Hey, stop. Let's see if that's the owner," I said. "We can talk to him now."

Jesse was a little hesitant, but he pulled into the parking lot. We went in and introduced ourselves to the owner. I recognized him right away.

"Are you in Rotary?" "Yes," he replied.

"Oh, me, too," I said. "I became a member not that long ago." Right away we had a great connection.

We asked about a lease, hoping it would be within what we could afford. It wasn't. We told him what we could afford, making it clear that we understood that it was a lot less than what he was asking. "If anything changes, please reach out to us," we told him.

As we started to leave, the conversation turned more personal. It turned out that we had just moved into the home he and his wife had lived in when they first moved to the town. His children's tiny handprints were in the concrete floor of our garage. He told us story after story about raising his kids in our home.

Because of the strong connection we had made, I was hopeful. A few days later, he called us. "I'm willing to let you kids have the space." He offered to take what we could afford and slowly increase the lease to the market rate over time. It was a dream come true.

There's no way we would have gotten the building if we followed the traditional protocol. If I had called the number on the "For Lease" sign and gone in to see it, we wouldn't have met the owner—we would have met the realtor he had hired to lease out the space. It felt like the universe was conspiring in our favor, guiding us through every twist and turn.

Meanwhile, I immersed myself in our community. We couldn't afford a membership at the local gym, but I swallowed my pride and volunteered at the gym's childcare center in exchange for a membership. I would strike up conversations with physicians and their spouses when they dropped off their children. This was invaluable because Jesse and I needed to get to know the physicians in the area in order to get referrals—the success of his practice would depend on those referrals. The gym seemed to be the common area where people connected.

I tried to get to know all the parents when they dropped off their kids. Over time, I befriended some of them. As I put myself out there, it felt as though the universe was working for our benefit. I couldn't believe how often I had opportunities to connect.

I was invited to join a book club with women who—initially—I declared to be way out of my league. I struggled with reading; I was barely able to read a whole book and understand what I read. So, it was a major stretch to put myself out there by joining them. Driving to the book club, I used to pray that no one would ask me to read anything out loud. Thankfully, no one ever did. However, we did engage in thought-provoking discussions, and I realized that we shared a passion for learning and personal development. Prodded by the book club, I became a much stronger reader and gained a belief that I belong anywhere I want to be. A few of these women still inspire me today to be amazing and continue to grow.

Throughout this time, I really wanted to have another baby. The doctor had given me the go ahead, but it took time. Of course, we had started trying to get pregnant right away, but—as so often happens in life—when you desperately want something, you learn patience. It took almost a year before we conceived our little Ella. I wish I could say that I was an example of patience, but I was not. I was soon impatient, and I nearly forgot about all the abundance in my life. A few short years before, I thought I was going to die. Now, I was frustrated because I didn't get my way immediately. I got pregnant only after I let go of having control and realized that if it was meant to be, then it would happen.

This little truth has been consistent in my life: If you want to have control, you need to learn how to let things go. We think we're in control. We set goals and plan missions and when things don't go our way, we lose our shit. We think, "Why is life not going the way it's supposed to?" I had a vision of getting pregnant, and when it didn't happen, I was pissed. Eventually, I thought, *whatever—if I'm supposed to get pregnant, it'll happen. If I don't get pregnant, we'll just keep living our life.*

After that, we got pregnant right away.

Ella was born the year we opened the clinic. Physical therapy practices are built on referrals. A patient sees their doctor, and the doctor refers them to a physical therapist. We built relationships with doctors, but if a doctor moved away or stopped referring patients to us, our referrals would be down overnight. At one point, we lost an orthopedist who was one of our main referral sources.

For the first several years, the clinic was a roller coaster ride. Jesse and I realized that our attitude and focus when business was up was very different from when it was down. When business was down, our language would change. We would go into a scarcity mindset and panic. We'd look at our budget to see where we could cut costs. During times of abundance, we were completely different. We were much freer with our finances, and we were much more positive. Our mindset, attitude, and conversations were more positive.

During the tough times, we decided to practice keeping our language and mindset positive. Over the next ten years, we had fewer downturns, and the downturns that came didn't last very long.

Putting two and two together, we realized that we can't avoid downturns in the economy and the business, but we *can* control our mindset. If things started to slow down, we didn't go on a budget. We determined that we wouldn't talk about the budget or money. We would just continue to live our life, and the money would come. We'd say, "The money will come. It's always come." We didn't say, "Where can we cut costs? Who do we need to let go?" We maintained a high standard for how we treated patients and our employees. We led with that.

And that's still how we operate today.

We also decided to spread our shallow roots wide. We added to our referral sources so we were drawing on a larger pool of people. Instead of depending on one doctor, we developed multiple referral sources. Now, if a doctor retires or closes his practice, it's a bummer—but we've got a host of other referral sources. So, we're constantly building the practice back up.

We've learned a great deal in our years in business. Eventually, we decided to get a second loan in order to hire more staff and get a bigger facility—we had outgrown our space. We got a second line of credit, got a larger space, and remodeled it. And that's where we are to this day.

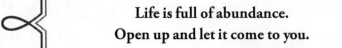

Life is full of abundance.
Open up and let it come to you.

We tend to focus on shiny objects but fail to recognize the abundance of the little things in life. You can have nothing and still feel like you have everything. When Jesse and I began our adult lives together, we had nothing. We had a baby and were living off of school loans. I was hospitalized with cardiomyopathy. We had no savings, and we were dependent on the state. It was a tough time for us.

But we were in love, we had our goals, and we had a young child who was the light of my world. I never felt poor. I never felt like we were less than others. I didn't feel like we didn't have what other people had—I knew we didn't, logically, but I didn't *feel* it. I felt like I had an incredible marriage. I felt like having our little boy was a great privilege. We lived in Arizona, and the sun was incredible. I loved everything about it. There was just so much to be thankful for.

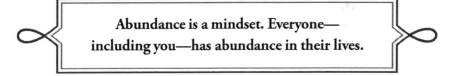

Abundance is a mindset. Everyone—including you—has abundance in their lives.

Being abundant depends on your focus. I don't live in fear. I don't want to give my energy to fear, so I focus on knowing that my financial, relationship, friendship, and health fears are taken care of through my faith.

To create abundance in my life, I focus on what I have. I am always grateful. Some days, I wake up on the wrong side of the bed. After all, I'm human. On those days, I focus on the fact that I'm alive, that I'm breathing, that my heart is beating, that I can walk, that I'm breathing without even thinking about it. I have an incredible body that somehow operates without me doing a damn thing. Some days, that's what I'm grateful for, and that's okay. If that's all you can be grateful for, start there. Start practicing with that. Remember what a miracle it is that you're alive, that you're here on earth today. Then, build from there.

Reflection Questions

What's blocking you from tapping into an abundance mindset?
1.

2.

3.

What do you need to do to clear your blocks and tap into an abundance mindset?

Personal Reflections:

Part 2:

Thought

"The mind is everything. What you think, you become."
—Buddha

Our thoughts are the stories we tell ourselves about our experiences. Whether those stories are limiting or liberating depends on our mindset. Our thoughts shape our reality, and they have the power to create the life we want or hold us back. To truly understand our thoughts, we must become observers of our mind and learn to detach from our inner chatter.

CHAPTER 5:

Dream Big

When you live your life linearly, you tend to go from the same to the same. You seldom seek out new experiences and stay away from opportunities to grow. Settling for a monotonous job, maintaining unfulfilling relationships, or neglecting personal interests and passions. Your life is the same every day; you're on autopilot. There's not much going on; you're just *existing*.

When we opened the clinic, the kids were little. We were working all the time. I would drop my kids off at a friend's house; she would help them do their homework, and I would go to work. One day, I pulled into my driveway and realized I didn't even remember the drive home. That scared me, because my babies were in the car.

Wow, I thought, *I'm not present. I am just a body in motion.*

It was go time for the clinic, and we had gotten sucked into autopilot.

Yikes, Katie, I thought, *you need to pay attention.* I needed to pay attention to *driving,* yes—but even more, I needed to pay attention to my *life.*

It was 2008—the middle of the real estate crash—and referrals were down at the clinic. We pulled money from anywhere we could to keep the clinic going. The last thing we wanted to do was lay people off. Everyone was scared about losing their home or their job—or both. People were leaving for other parts of the country, chasing better pay or better opportunities, walking away from their homes and starting over elsewhere.

We were at a crossroads once again. We took out a second mortgage on our home to keep the clinic going, but we were rapidly approaching the point where we couldn't keep everything afloat. I'd reached out to our bank multiple times to see if we could adjust our payment until things settled down. If you lived that recession, I don't have to tell you that the bank wasn't interested in my story.

One day, in this state of scarcity, I was grocery shopping with a friend. We chatted as we walked the aisles. I grabbed some mayonnaise.

"Ugh," I said. "I hate this brand. It tastes fake to me." My friend smiled at me. "Then why are you buying it?"

"It's the cheapest one, and in case you haven't noticed, we don't have any money. We're losing everything, including our home."

"I know," she said, "But look at the price difference between that one and the one you like. What is it—30 cents?"

I looked. "Yeah."

She smiled at me again. "Katie, you're worth 30 cents. Get the mayonnaise you like."

It sounds silly, but that moment in the store changed me forever. I was feeling utterly defeated. We had put in so much work and made so many sacrifices to buy our home and build up the clinic, and we were close to losing it all. The idea of starting over with nothing was so daunting, like facing an impossibly high mountain. But when my friend told me I was worth 30 cents, I felt like I was worth something.

Yes, I'm worth 30 cents. I grabbed the mayonnaise, put it in the cart, and smiled. I replayed that moment over and over in my mind for the next week. Because of the challenges we were facing, I had lost not only my abundance mindset but also my belief that I was worthy.

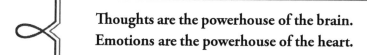

**Thoughts are the powerhouse of the brain.
Emotions are the powerhouse of the heart.**

This realization swept through me like lightning. I was suddenly reminded that I *am* worthy and so is my family. I brought my focus back to our future and away from our current situation.

I visited our attorney one last time to see if there was anything else we could do to keep our home. He advised us that all we could do was wait for the bank to reach out. So, I focused my thoughts and energy on big dreams.

I dreamed that the clinic would turn around, that referrals would pick up again.

I dreamed that we would find a home in the countryside, where the kids could run free outside. On the weekends, we drove around looking at homes in the country, imagining our family living in one of them.

We didn't worry about the *how*; we focused on what we wanted.

That year, we lost two homes—the one we lived in and the one we had purchased. But we saved our clinic. We quit paying our mortgage so we could pay our employees. When the bank fore-closed, I knew we would find another home one day, the dream home we had always wanted. I was dreaming big and visualizing it.

Because of our commitment to our community and involve-ment in multiple organizations, we had a great group of friends. One friend knew we were losing our home, but he also knew we were hard workers who would get things turned around in no time.

He also happened to be in the business of private lending. One day he told us he'd consider loaning us the money to get into a home.

Before my friend's mayonnaise comment got our mindset turned around, we weren't people you'd want to lend money to. We were in a state of lack. We gave off desperate energy. We complained and felt sorry for ourselves. Now, something had shifted in us, and our friend—perhaps consciously, perhaps not—saw the change. Otherwise, he never would have offered such a gift.

He and his lending partner shared their terms with us. At first, I thought, *we'll never come up with the down payment.* But I caught myself and quickly changed my mindset.

"We can do this," I told Jesse. "I'm not sure *how,* but I think we can do it."

The first thing that needed to fall into place was for business to pick up at the clinic so Jesse could take a paycheck again. We rolled up our sleeves and did all the things we hated. I brought coffee to the doctor's offices and practically begged them to send us refer-rals. We attended every community event we could. We went to every charity event we were invited to, knowing we couldn't actu-ally bid on anything. We swallowed our pride and held our heads high. Although we didn't have much, we knew we were worthy, and we had a big dream.

Soon, Jesse was bringing home a consistent check once again, and I started saving like a crazy person. We tightened our budget and sold things—but we did it from a mindset of abundance, not out of lack. We knew every penny was moving us toward our dream home.

After a year, we had saved enough to start looking for a new home. One day Jesse was out fishing with a friend, and they drove by a place he thought was worth looking at. I loaded up the kids and drove out to see it. My intention was to just drive by, but when I arrived, I pulled into the driveway. To my dismay, a car pulled in behind me.

I was so embarrassed. I knew I wasn't supposed to drive up to a home without an appointment and without our agent. But I was stuck—there was no place to turn around.

I rolled down my window. "I'm so sorry," I told the woman in the other car. "I'll leave and make an appointment."

The woman was so kind. "No way," she said. "You're here already. Just come in and see the house."

We spent the next hour hanging out and chatting about the home. The kids and I fell in love with it. We knew this was our home—until I asked what their asking price was. I pretended everything was okay, but I was so disappointed—we couldn't afford it.

"Thank you so much," I said as we were leaving. "I really appreciate your time. I don't think we'll be able to make an offer right now, though. Good luck."

"Well, why don't you offer what you can and let us see," she told me. "Okay," I replied.

At home, Jesse and I talked. Then we called our agent and made an offer. To our surprise, we got the home. It was our dream home—the one I'm living in today, where I finished raising our babies, and where I'm writing this book. Our kids grew up playing outside in the woods, raising animals, watching the stars, and so much more. And it all happened because one day in the grocery store, my friend told me I was worth 30 cents, and I believed her. My big dream happened because I'm worth it.

Our lives changed drastically, and it all stemmed from asking, "Aren't I worth 30 cents?" That question triggered a one percent shift in my mind. I started questioning everything in my life. I realized I was worth more. When I want more, I think, "What do I have to do to achieve my dreams?" Thinking big and believing has changed my life.

Your mindset matters. Everything in life starts with a thought. Whether you recognize it or not, your daily thoughts are moving you toward an end result. If you live on autopilot, you may end up somewhere without understanding how or why you got there. It's important to dream big and understand how your thoughts move you toward your dreams.

I check the direction of my thoughts every day, when I get up in the morning and when I go to bed at night. Most people don't pay any attention to their thoughts, but we should. There's a machine upstairs between our ears that runs the show, and we need to give it energy, conscious attention. Conscious thought is the starting point for dreaming big. Achieving our big dreams in life, stretching ourselves to reach them, starts with paying attention to our thoughts.

Start paying attention to your thoughts. Can you see where your thoughts are taking you? What patterns are showing up? If your thoughts are negative, you'll see negative things happen in your life. If your thoughts are positive, you'll find that, most of the time, positive things happen. If you pay attention to your thoughts, you'll start connecting the dots. If you consciously dream big, you can move forward to achieve your lofty goals.

Dreaming big gives you the opportunity to stretch yourself.

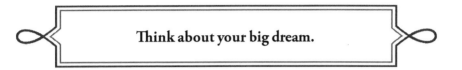

Think about your big dream.

One of my big dreams was to fly first class.

When I was 19, just after Jesse and I got married, his best friend—worked for Delta—gave us a pair of airline buddy tickets. When we flew, they bumped us to first class. I remember feeling so special when the flight attendant brought warm cloth towels for us to clean our hands.

After that, I dreamed of someday being able to fly like that again. We always flew economy, but I kept the dream alive. Every time I walked past first class to my economy seat, I would say to myself, "One day I will fly first class again."

When we booked a trip to Fiji last year, we got bumped up to first class. That was even more special than the first experience, because it was an international flight. I loved every minute of it. I'll never forget the joy I felt getting into my big, roomy seat. I wrapped a blanket around my legs and made myself cozy. The flight attendant brought us champagne and welcomed us to the flight. I was giddy. I smiled at Jesse and thought, *Wow, this is our life*. I couldn't stop smiling; it was a dream come true.

It proved to be everything I thought it would be. The flight attendants catered to our every desire. I still can't get over how comfortable our seats were—they laid completely flat and enveloped us like little cocoons. Truly, the best way to fly.

My favorite part of flying first class was the feeling of rest I had when we got to our destination. We were ready to hit the ground running—it was like we had bought ourselves *time*, because we didn't have jet lag. We were able to enjoy our destination immediately, and when we came home it was the same—we didn't have to take time off work to readjust. I wish everyone could fly that way.

For someone else, flying first class might not be a big dream. But for me, it was. When I set the intention to fly first class years ago, I didn't know how to achieve that dream. It's important to see that dreaming big isn't about knowing how to achieve your goals. It's a matter of setting the intention and then consciously directing your daily thoughts to be in line with those goals.

I've been blessed with an incredible marriage. Some might say that it just happened that way, that I'm just a lucky person. However, that's not how life works. Our marriage is amazing because we've worked really hard at it. We've gone through multiple periods when we didn't think we would last and sought out marriage counseling.

One marriage counselor had us take a questionnaire. When she tallied the results, she said, "You guys literally could not be more opposite." She told us that she very rarely recommends divorce. "However, in your case," she said, "you should either consider divorce or be prepared for really hard work. It's very rare for such different people to find middle ground and create something worth having."

By now, you should have an idea how that landed for me. I guess I see everything in life as a challenge. When rough things happen or challenges come up, I think, *Why is this happening? How can this benefit me?* Then, I rise to the occasion—I pull up my sleeves and get to work.

My marriage is no different. To this day, there are times when I really can't stand my husband. He drives me absolutely batshit crazy. Although he couldn't be more different from me in so many ways, he's my best friend. He's the person I've chosen to do life with.

Jesse is amazing. His dedication to our family is unwavering, and the joy he exudes from taking care of us is beautiful. No matter what he's doing—whether he's bringing home an animal from a successful hunt, working in his office, growing food in his garden, gathering firewood to keep us warm, or any number of other things he does for us—his actions say, "I love you." His family means more to him than anything else. That's the man I love, the man I married.

The guy who didn't put the dishes away or didn't chop the onions my way is the same man. Those moments when he's doing something that drives me crazy—those are the pivotal moments in marriage, the moments when the work shows up. If I focus on some trivial thing he did or didn't do and allow myself to forget who he is, then I'm headed into a downward spiral.

He drives me crazy! How many times have I shown him how to chop the onions my way? Why doesn't he listen to me? Is it really that hard to just listen to me?

My mind will take the story on and on, leaving the current event and leaping back to yesterday's conversation when he wasn't really listening to me.

He cares more about that stupid phone than he cares about me.

If my brain is really on a roll, it will go way back in history and remind me of grievances from 20 years ago. I can be standing in the kitchen with the man I love and adore, and within five minutes of allowing my brain to go wild, I want a divorce.

Your thoughts control your life. I can also smile at Jesse when he doesn't cut the onions my way and remind myself of all the good in this man.

Hey, he's in the kitchen cooking with me!

I can shift my focus from what's happening at that moment to what I like about him. I can engage with him by asking about his day, taking my mind off the right way to cut the fucking onions. The key to having the marriage Jesse and I have is this choice. I'm not perfect, and sometimes I lose my shit about stupid stuff. But I've learned to stop the story before it gets too colorful. I bring myself back to the truth.

I live by this one question in my marriage: "Katie, what's true about this?" Anytime I'm having negative thoughts about or toward my husband, I ask myself this question. Every time, I come back to how amazing my husband is, to that person I fell in love with.

And yes . . . I have a bit of a control issue in the kitchen.

Reflection Questions

Wouldn't it be amazing if today . . . (Write down your big dreams.)

Personal Reflections:

CHAPTER 6:

Believe in Yourself

Opening the clinic with Jesse made me realize, "I can do anything I set my mind to, as long as I believe in myself."

We weren't in a perfect situation to open a clinic. I was a stay-at-home mom, taking care of Elijah. We had no savings, and Jesse was working a regular job. But I believed we could do it.

I've shared my belief in the power of visualization. But what I'm getting at here goes beyond visualization. It's a matter of having the desire within.

Napoleon Hill wrote, "You can be anything you want to be, if only you believe with sufficient conviction and act in accordance with your faith; for whatever the mind can conceive and believe, the mind can achieve." Anything is possible—you just have to believe and act.

I never thought we couldn't open a clinic—not for one moment. I believed we would work every day on moving forward. I believed we would do all the things we didn't want to do. I grew up with lack.

I saw people around me with nothing, and many of them did nothing about it. But I also saw people who had nothing that moved forward. The only difference was that those who moved forward got up and *did* something about their circumstances.

They got jobs and talked about what their lives would look like in the future. They didn't start out with anything more than those who were just waiting for their government assistance. But they *believed* in themselves. They believed they could change their lives, and that made all the difference.

I'm thankful every day that I know what it's like to have nothing and be nobody. That experience has been a tremendous gift, because out of it, I believe in my abilities and I have the strength to put myself out there. I know that if I fail, I'll be okay—because I've been at the bottom, and I was okay. I've felt great sadness, but I was okay; I've lost people, but I was okay; and I've been hurt, but I was okay. People who come from the kind of rough childhood I had have a huge advantage in life—their knowledge of what they can survive is far beyond that of those who've never struggled.

The first time I believed in myself was a time when I was in grave danger. I was spending the night at my aunt's house with my cousin. We were both sleeping in a hide-a-bed. I woke up in the middle of the night with a man on top of me and my vagina all wet. I had no idea what was going on. I froze.

The man whispered, "Don't worry. It's going to be okay. Go back to sleep."

I knew it wasn't going to be okay, and I couldn't go back to sleep. My cousin was right next to me. Before then, every time I had been molested, I was alone. But this time was different—this time my cousin was next to me, and she was younger than me.

I had a moment of belief that I was powerful and that I could make it stop. So I did—I jumped out of the bed, crying and telling the man to leave me alone and stop talking to me. My aunt heard me crying and immediately came to my rescue. All hell broke loose.

I will never forget that moment. There are moments in life where you become superhuman. That was my first experience of knowing my power and strength. That realization of my power and strength has carried me through many situations. It taught me that I matter. I have power. I believe in myself, and I *can*.

My children sometimes struggle with believing in themselves or feelings of unworthiness. Generally, I think it's because they didn't have to struggle as they were growing up. They sometimes think they have to hit rock bottom or lose everything in order to know what they're capable of. What would serve them best is to learn from someone else's experience, to believe what others share.

Sometimes we need someone to remind us to believe in ourselves. Awhile back, I attended a Tony Robbins event. We were divided into small groups of six, and in some small groups like that you get to know people pretty well.

After one exercise to help us tap deeper into ourselves, a woman in the group came up to me. "I really like your energy," she said. "You make me feel so strong and powerful. I'm just wondering if you'd be willing to coach me."

At the time, I worked as a realtor and occasionally helped Jesse out at the clinic. "Oh, I'm not a coach," I told her. Looking back, I think I've been a coach my whole life. But I didn't recognize my power at that moment, and I didn't believe in myself as a coach.

The woman didn't give up, though. She kept asking me to coach her until I agreed. She helped me find coaching as an outlet to fuel my soul and help other people.

You don't have to struggle to believe in yourself and your ability. Learn from others; believe their pain and their struggle. Believe *me* when I say, you are a badass. You *are*.

Your life depends on you and no one else. Your successes and failures are 100% yours—there are no external circumstances. You can be your best advocate or your worst enemy. But you are invincible when you believe in yourself.

Reflection Questions

What situations or events make it hard for you to believe in yourself?

1.

2.

3.

What do you need to do to begin to believe in yourself more?

Personal Reflections:

CHAPTER 7:

Remember What You Want

We live in a world where everybody wants to know what their *why* is. Why am I here? Why am I doing what I'm doing? Why does it matter?

I titled this chapter "Remember What You Want" because I think it's easier to understand what you want than it is to answer a big question like "Why?"

My kids are grown and gone. Elijah called yesterday. He's in the military, in training; the training he's in can put me in a place of sadness and fear. I have to remind myself what I want—I want my son to be happy, and he's doing what he wants to do.

There are many crossroads in life. I've come to many—during the growth of our physical therapy practice, a struggle with a friend, a moment when one of my children made a decision that deviated from what I wanted for them. Those were times when I had to focus on remembering what I wanted."

Recently, I was thinking about neither of my kids being in the area. It's sad for me; I miss them. In some families, all the kids stay in town. It's hard to see my family take a different direction. I have to keep asking myself, "What do you want? What's important to you?"

What's really important to me is that my kids become their best selves. It's not about me. It's about them growing and expanding and being the best version of themselves. It's easy for parents to get caught up in themselves and hold their kids back. It's not our place in life to hold our children back. But sometimes, it's what we do.

My kids are still part of my life. When I talked to Elijah yesterday, he told me about his training. It's intense; he's going through things that are unimaginable to me. Instead of reacting with sadness and fear or freaking out, I asked myself, "What do you want?" I want Elijah to be the best in his field. I want him to thrive. I want him to know that he can call me anytime, and I'll be there for him. I'll be available for him because I'm strong and I'm grounded. I'm his rock.

I must remind myself of these things.

Ella has an August birthday, so she graduated from high school as a 17-year-old. She informed Jesse and me that she wanted to travel to Germany after graduation for a few months. Of course, we were a bit apprehensive about our beautiful 17-year-old girl traveling to another country without us. I certainly wasn't overwhelmed with a warm and cozy feeling. My feelings were somewhere between, "Hell, yeah. Go and have the best time," and "Holy shit! What if something happens to her?"

As she was making the arrangements for the trip, I remember sitting on my bed and crying. I

wanted her to go on the trip, but I was terrified. I had to keep reminding myself of what I wanted.

I want my kids to grow into amazing adults, competent adults who can stand on their own two feet and take care of themselves.

I was at a crossroads.

Would I lean into the fear, as so many parents do?

Would I make it about me? I could say, "This is crazy, Ella. You can't do it." Would I focus on everything that could go wrong?

Or would I remember want I wanted?

I chose to focus on what I wanted. *She's going to have a magical time.* I reminded Ella (and myself) that most people are good. I focused on good stories. If someone shared a horror story about a girl traveling alone, I stopped them or changed the subject. I was diligent to stay focused on all that is good in the world.

The day she left, I hugged her tight, kissed her, and let my tears flow.

"You're a badass," I told her. "Have an awesome time. Enjoy every moment. And please—text me often."

She kissed me back and went on her way. She texted me the moment she landed. She was gone for nearly two months and, of course, had an amazing time. Friends—other parents— would ask me how I was doing, and I could honestly answer that I was doing well. Why?

Because I was focused on what I wanted and on all the good the world has to offer. That gave me real peace about her traveling.

Currently, Ella has decided not to go to college. I know I'm not the only parent working through this one. When I chose to bring Ella into this world, I did it with the intention of raising an adult who could think for herself, who would know how to learn and would search for growth. I never said, "Oh, and she'll go to college." Yet so many parents think they're a failure if their children don't go to college. I'm fighting that thought by remembering what my desired outcome is.

One of my girlfriends told me about an intention she set for her two boys—now ages 15 and 18—when they were babies. She was determined to raise them in an environment with a lot of diversity. She wanted them to travel and have opportunities to understand the world on a broad scale. At the same time, she wanted them to understand how small we are. She vividly remembers setting this intention for them. As they grew, she and her husband did what they could within their budget to travel, broaden the boys' horizons through books, and live a life of diversity.

When her 18-year-old son wanted to go on an international trip with people she didn't know, it was challenging for her to agree to it. There were so many unknowns—the environment, so many people she didn't know. She is an incredible mom who wants to be in the know. She needed to know the itinerary, the agenda, every detail.

On one hand, she didn't know how to say yes to the trip; on the other hand, she remembered her intention for her boys. She wanted her son to see the world in all its glory, beauty, and massiveness. When her son had this opportunity to gain that kind of experience, she wanted to say no, because it didn't match how she'd envisioned fulfilling her intention. She had envisioned the entire family traveling internationally together. In her mind's eye, she had never thought that she wouldn't be there *with* her son. She had to ask herself what she really wanted. What was the goal? When she thought about it, the goal was for her son to have this kind of experience. Then, the answer was obvious—let him go.

It's so important to remember our goals in life. Otherwise, we get wrapped up in our emotions— regret for the things we've done wrong, disappointment when things don't look the way we anticipated. We must keep what we want at the forefront of our minds. Today, my friend is thrilled that her son went on the trip. He had a wonderful experience, and she made it happen. She took the opportunity to grow, too. When she set the intention for her boys to grow up with diversity, she wanted to participate. Now, she's learned that when she sets a goal, she needs to be specific.

Her story is impactful because she set the intention early in her children's lives. Then, when an opportunity arose to fulfill that intention, she wanted to turn it down because it didn't fit in with what she'd pictured.

Have you ever rejected an opportunity to fulfill a goal because it didn't conform to your rules? It's so important to remember what you want. Keep asking yourself, "What do I want?" If you keep bringing the conversation back to what you want, you give yourself the best chance to land where you actually want to land.

Recently, we decided as a family to plan an extraordinary experience, something magical. Ella was turning 18, and Elijah was leaving to join the Air Force. We decided to go skydiving. I set the intention: I would jump out of the plane.

We sat down as a family multiple times and discussed what we expected from skydiving. I encouraged everyone to envision nothing but greatness, freedom, joy, and lightness. It was going to be amazing. It was going to be fun. It was going to be all the things we said it would be.

When we went, Elijah, Ella, and I all did exceptionally well. Jesse was terrified and had the most challenging time focusing on the positive. But he did well. I was so proud of him.

Before we went skydiving, we *chose* how we would experience it, how we would feel about it. We couldn't control things that might go wrong, so we didn't talk about those things. We focused on the feelings of joy we would have. Whatever else happened was supposed to happen.

On the day of our jump, we loaded up and started driving to the airport. The weather was bad, and we got a call from the skydiving company—our flight was in danger of being cancelled. We had been driving for quite a while, so we decided to just keep going. Maybe the weather would change. We had a great attitude about how the whole experience would turn out.

If we hadn't been intentional about what we wanted to experience, the phone call about possible cancellation of our jump would have landed very differently. We would have been disappointed; most likely, we would have turned around and gone home. We might have said, "This sucks.

We drove all this way for nothing. What a waste of time."

However, because we remembered our intention, we decided to continue. If the jump was meant to happen, it would. The point wasn't jumping out of the plane—it was planning the event together as a family. The point was the exhilaration and fear we'd feel jumping out of a plane together. Skydiving was a *tool* we were using to feel full of life, to push ourselves out of our comfort zone, to do something crazy freaking hard that scared the living hell out of us all.

It would have been easy to quit, to take the weather as a convenient excuse for not going through with it. But we remembered the intention we had set out, and we were all in. So, we continued on our way. As we arrived at the airport, the weather cleared, and we got to jump out of a plane together as a family.

Reflection Questions

What are some experiences you would like to have?

1.

2.

3.

How can you connect these experiences with remembering what you want?

Personal Reflections:

Part 3:

Emotions

"We cannot selectively numb emotions,
when we numb the painful emotions, we also
numb the positive emotions."
—BRENÉ BROWN

Emotions are the energy that moves through us. They are our body's way of responding to our thoughts and experiences. Emotions can be intense, uncomfortable, and even painful, but they are also essential for healing and growth. When we learn to embrace our emotions with openness and compassion, we can use them as a guide to uncover the deeper truths about ourselves and our lives.

CHAPTER 8:

Honor Your Feelings

One of the darkest moments in my life was when I had a mental breakdown.

My kids were teenagers, and I had spent most of my adult life raising them and proving to myself that I was in control of my emotions. I had direction in my life, and I knew what I was doing. I felt empowered and strong. I was working as a real estate agent and doing very well. The kids were doing well, and Jesse's clinic was thriving.

Then my mother's significant other of 20 years died suddenly. I didn't know him well and we were not close, my mother was devastated and, of course, I felt for her. My mother and I don't have a tight relationship, but my love for her has never wavered. When she hurts, so do I.

A few days after her partner died, we were all together at my brother's house. We wanted to have my mom over, make her some food, and love on her as best we could. Throughout the night, I felt myself getting pulled deeper and deeper into a very old feeling. I didn't recognize it at first. Throughout my adult life, I've worked on moving forward and forgetting the traumas of my past. Unfortunately, my body doesn't seem to forget as well as my brain.

I'd spent the evening with my mom. She seemed lost and scared. She cried on my shoulder for most of the night, whispering her sadness to me. I didn't realize it at first, but it brought me back to my childhood, to a moment when she was helpless. When the evening wrapped up, she started getting ready to leave. For some reason, I had thought she was going to stay at my brother's house for a few days.

"Where are you going?" I asked. Big mistake. Before she even answered, I knew where she was going. She was going to our old stepdad's house, to be with the man who had broken up our family years ago.

I already knew she spent time with him, but I was in a strange state that night, and the fact that she was going to his house hit me weirdly. The moment she walked out the door, I was transported back to my childhood—I was sitting on the street after family court, and she was leaving me to go be with him. A sense of abandonment crashed over me, and I lost control.

I had a glass in my hand, and I threw it at the ground. I started screaming bloody murder, pounding my fists against the wall. The tears came rushing like a massive waterfall. My whole world went black. I was crawling along the wall, trying to escape the pain.

My brother rushed over to grab me. "Leave me alone!" I yelled. "Don't touch me!" I started crying even harder.

Suddenly I awakened to what was happening and panicked. "Oh my God, don't let my kids see me this way," I told my brother, over and over.

My brother is much bigger and stronger than me; he grabbed me in a bear hug, and I melted. As I wept, a wave of shame came over me. I'd never allowed my guard down around my mom—and now I knew why.

My breakdown felt like somebody had cut my legs off. I was weak and confused. It felt like someone or something else had taken me over. I had a hard time accepting that the person acting that way was *me*. The hardest part for me to swallow was that it happened in front of my kids.

However, having my meltdown in front of my kids gave them a valuable lesson about honoring their feelings. I had talked with them about honoring our feelings, but we'd never talked about letting our feelings run their full course and not placing judgment on how long the process took.

What does it mean to honor our feelings?

How do we know when it's appropriate to move on from certain feelings? How do we ensure we're not cutting a feeling off too early?

Honoring our feelings isn't about hanging onto them for years and letting them control us. It's about giving them space to be seen and heard and then planning to move forward with new information.

For years, I thought I was honoring my feelings. I thought I was feeling them.

I would say things like, "I'm over that. It's not part of me anymore," or "I've dealt with that. I've seen the therapist; I've done the work."

In the weeks following my breakdown, my family and I discussed it. I worried that seeing me in such a state would negatively impact my children and husband. No mother or wife wants her loved ones to see her out of control. But because I thought I had been successfully managing my emotions, the situation felt even worse. I felt like I had deceived my family for years, pretending to be strong when I wasn't. The shame and guilt I felt were incredibly challenging.

But my kids told me that, although they disliked seeing me melt down, they were ultimately glad it happened. They knew I struggled with unresolved issues from my childhood, but they hadn't realized the depth of my strength until then. They didn't view me as weak, and they weren't ashamed of me. They certainly didn't think I had any reason to feel guilty. They told me I was the strongest person they knew and that the breakdown *needed* to happen. They believed I would be able to heal more profoundly now that I was free from hiding.

They were right. As I readjusted to my life, I noticed that I was breathing a little easier. It was as if I had been granted permission to feel sadness—an emotion I rarely allowed myself to experience.

In one conversation with my daughter, I shared my confusion about the breakdown. I had a positive attitude, and I was constantly working on my mindset. To all appearances, I was leading a successful life. I had happiness, wealth, healthy children, and a healthy marriage.

"But you may have never fully addressed the cycle of pain with your mother," Ella said. "You worked on controlling your mind, but what did you do to address your feelings?"

It was as if someone had hit me over the head with a frying pan. I worked so hard *not* to feel, rationalizing away my emotions, reminding myself of all the good in my life, and moving forward. It was an approach that brought me significant success, joy, and happiness. However, it was clear that I needed to allow myself to process the emotions from my childhood in a healthy way.

But how? Ella suggested that I take time for myself when I needed it, so I could let the cycle of emotions finish rather than suppressing them and moving on.

Now, if I wake up feeling sad, I perform my usual gratitude meditation and go for a walk. But I don't do these activities to make the sadness *disappear*. Instead, I *include* my sadness. I acknowledge it and invite it to join me on my walk. When I breathe, I breathe into the feeling and allow myself to experience it. I do the same with joy or happiness.

As I practiced this, I realized that I had been pushing away not just sadness but *all* my emotions. I worked hard to the perfect mom and perfect wife. Now, I'm grateful for my mental breakdown. By allowing myself to *feel*, I've become a much more complete person. I'm honest with my family about my emotional state, and for the first time, they get to see all of me. I'm *not* perfect, and that's wonderful. I'm *human*, and that's *much* better than being perfect.

Sometimes when I used to talk with my kids about their feelings, I'd say, "It's time for you to move on." It was like there was a time limit on how long they could feel those feelings, and then they needed to move on. After my breakdown, I realized that that's how I was living my life.

My daughter taught me to continue to feel my emotions until I don't feel them anymore. Honoring our feelings doesn't have an *outcome*. Saying, "I've done the work. I'm past that," is *not* honoring your feelings. But that was me—pushing things down and controlling them—until I got triggered. Then, because I *hadn't* truly honored my feelings, I had a full mental breakdown.

Why did I have that meltdown? If you had asked me if I was honoring my feelings, I would have said, "Yes. I know my dysfunctional childhood wasn't my fault. I know I'm a good person. I love myself. I'm kind. I'm a good mom." I would have given you any number of ways in which I thought I was honoring my feelings.

But I *wasn't* honoring my feelings, because as they came up, I explained them away. This is an important aspect of getting through the complete cycle of emotions. If a traumatic memory from my childhood came up in the middle of the night, I would tell myself, "Oh, Katie. You're past that. Just let it go."

When Ella suggested I take the time to complete the cycle of my emotions, I learned a valuable lesson. I thought I was honoring my emotions, but I was actually rationalizing them, locking them away in a dark room. Since that conversation with Ella, I've been slowing down and sitting with my feelings as they arise. I let them stay with me, without judging them or trying to change them. I honor them by acknowledging their existence.

Reflection Questions

What are some ways you can take care of yourself on a deep emotional level?

1.

2.

3.

What does it mean for you to honor your feelings?

Personal Reflections:

CHAPTER 9:

Take Care of Yourself

A s I'm writing this book, my children are beginning to create their own lives. Ella just left for an extended time in Europe, and Elijah just joined the Air Force. My children aren't little anymore. They're transitioning into adulthood.

I could dwell on my fear and anxiety about them leaving, but I endeavor to live in the moment and not worry. If I take care of myself at a deep level, I'm better able to be there for my family when they need me.

Before my kids left home, we planned a rafting trip on the lower Rogue River. Portions of the movie *The River Wild*, with Meryl Streep and Kevin Bacon, were filmed there. There are massive Class 5 rapids, ferocious and raging, and the mountains are stunningly beautiful. There's no cell service—you're unplugged from civilization, immersed in nature, and totally connected to the earth. Zane Grey wrote some of his work while in that area, and the cabin he lived in is still there. It's incredibly peaceful and serene, with all types of wildlife—eagles, bears, fish, and tiny critters.

The lower Rogue is somewhat frightening, because people die there every year when things go wrong on the huge rapids. You have to pay attention and be in the moment. On the raft, we had to work together as a family and trust, lean on, and take care of each other. It was an opportunity to express sincere love for each other. I planned the trip so we could enjoy an incredible journey together and experience everything the wilderness offered.

Sleeping outside under the stars and hoping the bears don't come by is a memorable experience. Elijah is a river guide, and it was great to see him in his element, sharing his gifts with us and leading us down the river. It was cool to watch my son lead my husband. Situations like that don't arise very often unless we're intentional about making them happen. Ella got to row through some rapids, too, and that boosted her confidence as a woman on the river.

The conversations we had and the time we spent together made me feel so full. Because my kids have left home, I'm feeling a certain level of sadness. Yet my sadness is taken care of, protected, and loved by my peace. I'm so full, because I created this experience. When I look back, I don't say, "Where'd the time go?" I look back and say, "What a wonderful experience we had!"

The trip was all about taking care of me. I love the outdoors; it fills my soul. Before the kids left, I wanted my family to have a deep connection. Even planning the trip and thinking about what we would experience allowed me to fill my soul.

What do you do to take care of yourself on an emotional level, deep in your soul? My family is everything to me. I wanted an experience that would fill me with love and gratitude, that would be a place I could go back to once the kids were off living their lives and becoming adults.

I pushed that trip selfishly. I knew we needed time alone together to bond, to create more memories. Because we took that trip, I am able to approach moments of heightened anxiety about the members of my family in a better way. I can be a rock for my family, because I got what I needed—I filled my cup with that experience.

If the rafting trip had only been for the benefit of my family—if it wasn't something I needed deep within my soul—it wouldn't have taken care of me emotionally. But it *was* for me, so I feel grounded. I feel strong. That doesn't mean I don't have mama moments when I don't hear from my son in the Air Force. But when his girlfriend calls me worried, crying, and scared, I have the emotional capacity to be there for her because I've taken care of myself.

We often think of self-care in terms of things like a trip to the spa. For me, a trip to the spa only fills my cup for a nanosecond; it doesn't fill me deeply. Take a moment to consider: What do you need to take care of yourself at a deeply emotional level?

The fruit of these kinds of experiences are tremendous. My kids are learning the importance of this kind of deep self-care. They realize that life is better when we make ourselves a priority. We can come together full, feeling good, able to share and be there for each other. Just think how much less stressed people would be if they took time to withdraw from our fast-paced tech-filled world and checked in with themselves, with their emotional well-being.

Our trip had many opportunities to fall apart, and part of the self-care was in the fact that we didn't let it fall apart. Self-care often means making sure the things that are important to you *happen*. It's not always about taking a warm bath.

As my family transitions into a new phase, we're all full of joy, peace, love, and excitement for each other. We're planning our next journey.

Self-care for me and my family isn't just a physical consideration—working out and eating well. It's also a matter of fulfilling emotional needs. This aspect of self-care is so important, but we tend to neglect it. Through this kind of self-care, I'm not worried and anxious about my kids leaving. I created space for us to make beautiful memories, memories that are now sustaining me.

Reflection Questions

What can you do on a consistent basis to take care of yourself on a deep emotional level?

1.

2.

3.

What do you need to do to make this happen?

Personal Reflections:

Part 4:

Actions

"We are what we repeatedly do.
Excellence, then, is not an act, but a habit."
—ARISTOTLE

Actions are the tangible expressions of our thoughts, beliefs, and emotions. They are the way we engage with the world and create our reality. Our actions have the power to uplift or diminish others, and they reflect our inner state. When we act from a place of authenticity and integrity, we can create positive change and make a meaningful impact on the world around us.

CHAPTER 10:

Level Up

We are always looking for ways to move forward and level up. Leveling up is the process of acquiring new skills, meeting new people, acquiring knowledge, or experiences in order to enhance our abilities, reach personal goals, or improve the overall quality of our lives. If you want to level up, keep looking up. Look at the horizon and ask, "Where am I going?"

When I was a senior in high school, I applied to become a Rotary foreign exchange student. This program offered students nine months to live in a different country. I saw it as a way to leave my house, have an adventure, and strike out on my own.

In Oregon, each Rotary district designates funds to send a high school student abroad as an ambassador of the United States and Rotary. Rotary exchange students are selected through an interview process where a selection committee interviews candidates, then vets them.

Candidates that are selected participate in a nine-month training program. Part of the training program involves meeting other exchange students in the state. The exchange students also learn about their destination countries, communication skills, how to handle loneliness and depression, and how to handle being immersed in a different culture.

The students are then assigned to one of their top three destinations. When training is complete, they go abroad and live with three different families in their host country. They attend school in the host country, living with a host family, fully immersed in a foreign culture.

Rotary views these exchange students as ambassadors for America. They're high-caliber people with good character and morals. The idea behind the exchange program is that the more we understand other cultures, the more we can agree on things and spread love throughout the world. For example, if I know and love someone in Germany and something terrible happens there, I'll relate very differently to that situation than I would if I wasn't connected to a German friend. The idea is to make our large world smaller, to bring people together.

I went through the entire interview process, was selected, and began the training program. When the time came to be assigned to a country, I was assigned to go to Mexico. I had been to Mexico a couple of times on mission trips with our church and I was really looking forward to experiencing other parts of the world. Mexico was not one of the destinations I had chosen. I was so disappointed and angry. But instead of speaking up and letting someone know, I ran away. I sabotaged the entire experience because I didn't know how to have a conversation to stand up for myself and share my feelings.

Looking back, I was a young girl trying to live in a new world. The world that I had left didn't provide me with wonderful opportunities to travel the world. It sounded good to me to be a high school exchange student; I saw other kids do it, and I thought, *my gosh, you can go move to another country for a year and get the hell out of here.* I was always looking for a way out of whatever situation I was in.

Going through the training, I felt stupid. I had to read and speak in public, and that put pressure on me. I didn't want to let my dad down, so I kept going. But when it was time to leave, I panicked and ran away. I didn't know what else to do. Even though I leveled up into new territory and gained new skills, through the Rotary program my feelings didn't change—I still felt like I didn't belong.

When I came home after running away, I was behind in school. My counselor told me I needed to catch up if I wanted to graduate. I buckled down, graduated, and moved on to college.

That was my next experience of leveling up. I was the first person in my family to go to college and I decided not to stay in my hometown. Instead, I went to Western Oregon State University in Monmouth, Oregon, near Portland.

The school's housing administrators assigned me to live with eighteen other females. I thought, *Holy shit, there's no way I can do that.* I don't have any sisters, I don't particularly like girls, and I didn't want to share space with anyone.

I wanted to live by myself. So, I called the school and said, "Hey, is there any way I can have my own room?"

"Sure," said the voice on the other end of the line. Then they told me how much it would cost. I didn't have that much money.

"Is there any way I can get my own room without having to pay for it?"

"Actually, yes, there is." The way to do it was to take a job giving tours to incoming students every Thursday. If I did that, I could have a room all to myself in the dorm. I wouldn't have to share with anyone.

"Sweet! Sign me up," I said.

They told me not to get my hopes up. "A lot of people apply for this job . . . "

I applied anyway. I visualized myself in my own room. I just saw it as done. I *had* to have my own room in order to go to college. I got called in to meet with the people in charge of hiring the tour guides. There wasn't a sit-down interview, per se. They described the job and asked if I was interested if I could see myself in that role. I'm sure *they* were paying attention, but I don't remember the details. I wasn't visualizing myself walking around campus as a tour guide—I was visualizing myself in my own room.

I wasn't particularly concerned with the *how*; I was focused on having my own room. I didn't think it was my job to figure out how it would happen. I just knew that I was going to have my own space. The stronger image in my mind was me sitting in my room, not me giving tours. Sure enough, I got the job, got my own room that I didn't have to share with anyone. It was absolutely perfect.

My high school and college years were a time of growth, and I have no regrets about my experiences during that time. In those years, I learned that if you want to get somewhere in life, you have to find people who are ahead of you and start doing what they're doing. Start learning and gaining new skills.

My point in relating these stories is that we should always look for ways to level up. You won't necessarily take every opportunity that comes along, but you should keep moving forward. I've learned that I can do whatever I want to do. I'm in control. Taking a risk and trying things outside my comfort zone has taught me that I'm in control of my opportunities and where they go. If you learn and apply what you learn, you'll be in control of your life, your emotions, and your choices. I don't feel bad about missing the exchange program—it wasn't for me. But I learned a hell of a lot about myself by applying and going through the process. It caused me to grow.

Reflection Questions

List some things you'd like to experience that are out of your comfort zone?

1.

2.

3.

What do you need to do today to start moving out of your comfort zone?

Personal Reflections:

CHAPTER 11

Live Consciously

Expanding and growing your life takes conscious effort. It takes action. Making a conscious effort to create the life you want takes work.

But here's a counterintuitive challenge. If you *don't* take control of your life and *don't* make choices that get you into action, you're still going to have to work. You'll just be doing a different kind of work.

Let's use parenting as an illustration.

Peggy and Peter Jones have two children, and they both have full-time jobs. Peggy is a real estate agent and Peter is an accountant. Before having children, they had an active social life and traveled often. Now, their social life centers around their children. Everything they do is intentional. They are present for family time and weekends. They encourage their children to play sports and participate in the arts, and they support them at all their events. Every year, they plan a family trip and involve the children in coming up with their activities. They all discuss the fun places they're planning to visit. Peggy and Peter don't have much adult time with their friends. They're focused on their family. They've set up a structure and boundaries for their children to have success.

Marsha and Matthew Smith also have two children. They've always had a very active social life, and they travel extensively. Marsha is a real estate agent and Matthew is an accountant. When they had their kids, they decided not to change how they were living; they planned to take things as they came. They wanted their kids to go with the flow. They don't act with intention when it comes to the direction their kids should take, and they don't provide the kids with life experiences that enrich them. They're just *existing*—taking life as it comes. There aren't any structures or set boundaries for the children. One of them has started getting into trouble at school, but Marsha and Matthew think it's a phase he'll outgrow.

There is no perfect way to raise kids, and as parents, we always strive to do our best. While there is no definitive right or wrong approach, investing time and effort in our kids, especially when they are young, greatly increases the likelihood of positive outcomes. Parents who prioritize their children's upbringing in the early years lay a solid foundation for smoother parenting experiences when their kids reach their teenage years. The experiences of these two groups of parents are vastly different. There really is no guarantee. But there is a better probability that if you put the time up front when the kids are little you will have less of a challenge that may be faced by parents who didn't invest time and effort early on.

When raising kids, the goal is to equip them with the necessary tools to navigate challenges as adults. This includes fostering the ability to make positive choices, thinking independently, and cultivating strong self-esteem. When my kids were little, I made it a priority to provide guidance and empower my children with these tools and many other tools that would make them independent adults. Now, as young adults, they are actively building their own lives. Instead of asking me what to do when faced with challenges, they reach out to share with me how they are going about tackling the challenge. I am now able to be on the other side of parenting where I offer support by listening and providing guidance, and consciously being there for them without imposing my opinions or enabling them.

The point is, no matter what choices you make—Path A or Path B—either one will work. But at some point, along either path, you'll be working your ass off. So, why not choose the *conscious* path, which gives you the opportunity to create the life you want for yourself.

Living consciously with others often involves working together towards a common goal. As parents it is our responsibility to guide our children into adulthood where they get the opportunity to share their gifts with others. This is our core purpose as human beings is to share our gifts with others. When you gather with other humans, you start to allow yourself to open up.

Recently, I went on a trip with 13 beautiful entrepreneurial women. I met one of these women in a Tony Robbins mastermind. I had joined the mastermind for the sake of personal business development, and here was this amazing woman who reached out to me and we became fast friends. She is the ultimate connector and understands the power of Shallow Roots system. The Shallow Roots system is implementing the power of human connection. The more "roots" we put out and the broader we spread, the more connected we are to the world. The more connected we become with the world the more resources are available for us to create, grow and expand the life we want.

This group of like-minded women are committed to living life in a forward moving direction. Every year we get together and take a trip to be with each other, have fun, and support one another.

We don't think of ourselves as having a "mastermind," in the sense of the word, even though we support each other immensely. Some masterminds focus on spiritual growth; others focus on business growth. Group members may be at different stages in their growth, but they want to stay connected and support each other. In our time together we share our knowledge and learn from one another. On our most recent trip, as always, when we arrived at our destination, we spent time catching up. After a couple days, layers of insulation started peeling off, because we were getting comfortable with each other and asking deep questions around the dinner table—questions such as:

How do you show up in the world? Who are you?

How do you participate?

What's your role here?

How are you playing the game of being a human?

By the end of the last day, everyone understood their role. No one's role was better or more important—we realized that everyone's role is important. Everyone has a superpower.

Participating in the world isn't a competition; it's about showing up and saying, "This is the human that I am, these are the innate gifts I've been blessed with, and this is what I have to offer."

For example, if you're going through a hard time and tell me about it, it takes *zero* work for me to listen to you and repeat what you told me using a different theme. That's my superpower—I'm a reframe coach.

How do you show up?

What do you do that you get positive feedback about?

As you consider these questions, you may suddenly realize, "Oh—this is my calling. This is what I'm supposed to do."

When humans come to that kind of realization, and they do it together, magic happens. I see more than *my* gift, *my* offering—I see so many offerings all around me, and we're all supporting each other, lifting each other up, and helping each other reach higher levels of energy. It's not a competition where we compare to see whose gift is better, more special, or more important.

Sometimes my gift is needed; sometimes, it takes a backseat to yours.

On that recent trip with my business besties, every woman brought a superpower to the table. One woman held a search engine optimization class for social media. I did mini one-on-one sessions on reframing. Another woman gave a presentation on investing. While another one explained to us our relationship with food and gave us tools on how to have a better relationship with it. That's how we show up and participate— everyone sharing their superpower.

That's how I live my daily life. I show up asking, "What's good about this?" and "How can I help you? How can I contribute?" It's beautiful to watch a group of humans collaborate in this way, acting without hidden agendas, acting out of pure love.

Reflection Questions

What do you need to do to start living more consciously aware?

1.

2.

3.

How will you start today to make this happen?

Personal Reflections:

CHAPTER 12:

Participate as a Human: Grow the Life of Your Dreams

In this book, I've shared my stories. You have a sense of the pain of the situations and experiences I went through. I was able to turn my life around, because I realized that my life was up to *me*.

Participating as a human starts with you. It starts with sharing the best of yourself—first, within yourself, and then with others.

How do you participate as a human? How do you live your life?

Do you see opportunities around you? Are you grateful for the little things?

Our attitudes, thoughts, emotions, and actions allow us to create, grow, and expand the life we desire.

We are always evolving, always growing. Situations arise to take us out of our comfort zone and allow us to experience new ways of doing and being.

Taking responsibility for your life begins with self-awareness. It requires you to understand your strengths, weaknesses, values, and aspirations. By being aware of your own thoughts, emotions, and behaviors, you can gain clarity about what you want.

Rather than being passive or reactive, adopt a proactive mindset. Take initiative, seek opportunities, and actively pursue personal growth and development. Instead of waiting for things to happen, take the driver's seat in your own life. Recognize that every choice you make, no matter how small, contributes to the overall trajectory of your life. Challenges and obstacles are inevitable, but when you view them as learning experiences and persevere through them, you'll develop resilience and evolve as an individual.

This chapter is dedicated to you, the reader.

No one achieves success in this world all on their own. Sure, there are some people who have comparatively little need for other people, but overall, people need people. We participate as humans by connecting, ensuring that others are seen, and allowing ourselves to be seen. That's how we support our village and create, grow, and expand together.

PARTICIPATE AS A HUMAN:

Grow the Life of Your Dreams

Use the journal on the following pages to connect your thoughts on each part of the book so you can begin to create, grow, and expand the life you desire.

Part 1: Attitude

Chapter 1: Maintain an Attitude of Gratitude

Exercise: Write down three things you're grateful for today. Reflect on why they matter to you and how they positively impact your life.

Chapter 2: Take Responsibility

Exercise: Think of a recent situation where things didn't go as planned. Write down what role you played in the outcome and how you can take responsibility to improve future situations.

Chapter 3: Be Curious: Ask Questions

Exercise: List three areas of your life where you'd like to learn more. Write down at least two questions related to each area that you can explore further.

Chapter 4: Be Abundant
Exercise: List five personal strengths or resources that contribute to your abundance. Reflect on how you can utilize them to manifest more abundance in your life.

Part 2: Thought

Chapter 5: Dream Big

Exercise: Write down your biggest dream, no matter how unrealistic it seems. Then, list three smaller goals that will help you work toward achieving your big dream.

Chapter 6: Believe in Yourself

Exercise: Write a letter to your future self expressing your belief in your ability to overcome obstacles and achieve your dreams.

Chapter 7: Remember What You Want

Exercise: Create a vision board, physically or digitally, that represents your goals and desires. Put it somewhere where you'll see it every day so it will remind you of what you want.

Part 3: Emotions

Chapter 8: Honor Your Feelings

Exercise: Reflect on an emotion you've experienced recently. Write down the situation that triggered it and acknowledge the validity of that emotion without judgment.

Chapter 9: Take Care of Yourself
Exercise: Schedule 15 minutes of "Me" time every day for the next week. During your "Me" time, engage in activities that help you feel connected to your inner self, such as meditation, journaling, or spending time in nature.

Part 4: Actions

Chapter 10: Level Up
Exercise: Reflect on a past failure or challenge that ultimately led to personal growth. Identify the area of your life where this growth occurred and write down the key lessons you learned from that experience.

Chapter 11: Live Consciously

Exercise: For one week, practice mindfulness by intentionally focusing on the present moment during daily activities. At the end of the week, write down any changes you notice in your thoughts, emotions, or overall well-being.

Chapter 12: Participate as a Human

Exercise: Commit to participating in a community event or volunteering for a cause you're passionate about. Write down the details of the event or cause and reflect on how your participation has enriched your life and connected you with others.

THANK YOU FOR READING MY BOOK!

My mission is to help others create, grow, and expand their life. Here is how you can help me spread that message:

- Leave a review on Amazon.
- Share the book with a friend.
- Send me an email and share your story with me.

ACKNOWLEDGMENTS

First and foremost, I would like to thank my children. Your relentless faith in me and your insistent reminder that we are here to lift one another up has been the fuel to my fire. It's because of you that I found the courage to begin anew, and it's your push that continues to propel me forward.

When the weight of silence was heavy, you reminded me of the importance of voicing our stories.

To my husband, who took a chance on a 15-year-old girl who was on a steep learning curve, thank you. Your unwavering love and support have been the pillars of my strength, especially during those moments when I felt utterly depleted. Your constancy, your faith in our journey, and your constant presence have been my rock.

To my siblings, each of you holds a unique place in my heart. Scott, my older brother, and Tiffany, my sister-in-law, your ceaseless support throughout the various phases of my life has been my beacon. You've always been my constant, and for that, I am eternally thankful. To my younger brothers, Robbie and Matthew, your presence in my life has been a saving grace. When we were young, your mere existence impelled me to be a better version of myself, if only to be a pillar for you. This drive has never left me, and for that, I am eternally grateful. I love you all dearly.

To my mother-in-law, the epitome of maternal love, thank you. Your entrance into my life was not a coincidence, but a perfectly timed intervention. The unconditional love you've showered upon me is a gift that I will forever cherish.

A heartfelt thanks to my parents, who surpassed their own upbringings to provide me with a better foundation. Their efforts to evolve into better people, their constant encouragement, and their ceaseless faith in me are deeply recognized and appreciated.

I have been blessed with an expansive family, and there are countless others whose contributions have shaped me and, in turn, this book. While it's impossible to mention everyone, please know your influence and support have not gone unnoticed.

Specifically, I would like to express my deep gratitude to Crea. Without your belief in me, your unwavering support, and your constant availability, this book might have remained a dream. Thank you for being there through the full spectrum of emotions – the tears, the laughter, the frustrations, and the triumphs. Your role in this journey is more significant than you know.

Lastly, to Cheli, your patience, your kind words, and your boundless love and support have been invaluable. You have been a guiding light throughout this process, and for that, I am profoundly grateful.

In the creation of a beautiful life, and indeed this book, community has been my backbone. Your support, love, and faith have brought this book to life, and I am endlessly thankful for your presence on this journey. I am privileged and humbled to count you all as my community.

Thank you all.

END NOTES

Chapter 1
Louse Hay, *You Can Heal Your Life*, (Carlsbad, CA, Hay House, 1984).

Part 3
Brené Brown, The Gifts of Imperfection. (New York, NY, Random House, 2020).

Chapter 6
Napolean Hill, *Think and Grow Rich*, (Reprinted by Hawthorne Books, 1972) Original Copyright 1937 by The Napoleon Hill Foundation.

ABOUT THE AUTHOR

Katie Elliott is an author, life coach, and a true believer in the power of the human spirit. Born in 1979, her early life was marked by chaos and upheaval, including sexual abuse and abandonment. Despite these challenges, Katie persevered and discovered the tools to create a beautiful life for herself. Now, as the author of *From Shallow Roots*, she's sharing these tools with others so they, too, can find the path to healing and growth.

In addition to her work as an author and life coach, Katie has excelled in various other areas of her life. She has been married to her high school sweetheart, Jesse, for nearly 25 years and has two beautiful children, Elijah and Ella. Katie helped her husband establish and assists in the running of his physical therapy clinic. She's also been a successful real estate agent.

Katie's philosophy on life is one of openness, understanding, and compassion. She believes that everything in life can be a win–win with the right mindset and that human connection is one of the most powerful forces in the world. She finds joy in observing how people live and interact with each other. Katie loves to travel, fish, cook, and laugh, and she knows that life is meant to be enjoyed to the fullest.

Through *From Shallow Roots* and her work as a life coach, Katie is committed to helping others realize their full potential and create the beautiful life they deserve. Her own life is a testament to the power of resilience, perseverance, and a deep appreciation for the joys of living.

Made in the USA
Middletown, DE
05 September 2023

37591899R00083